# DICKENS
# DALI
# & OTHERS

## Other Books by George Orwell

DOWN AND OUT IN PARIS AND LONDON

BURMESE DAYS

A CLERGYMAN'S DAUGHTER

KEEP THE ASPIDISTRA FLYING

THE ROAD TO WIGAN PIER

HOMAGE TO CATALONIA

COMING UP FOR AIR

INSIDE THE WHALE AND OTHER ESSAYS

THE LION AND THE UNICORN

ANIMAL FARM

NINETEEN EIGHTY-FOUR

SHOOTING AN ELEPHANT AND OTHER ESSAYS

SUCH, SUCH WERE THE JOYS

THE ORWELL READER

THE COLLECTED ESSAYS, JOURNALISM AND LETTERS
OF GEORGE ORWELL (4 vols.)

A COLLECTION OF ESSAYS

# GEORGE ORWELL

# DICKENS, DALI & OTHERS

**A HARVEST/HBJ BOOK**
**HARCOURT BRACE JOVANOVICH, PUBLISHERS**
SAN DIEGO NEW YORK LONDON

# NOTE

MOST of these essays have appeared in print before, and several of them more than once. "Charles Dickens" and "Boys' Weeklies" appeared in my book, *Inside the Whale*. "Boys' Weeklies" also appeared in *Horizon*, as did "Wells, Hitler and the World State," "The Art of Donald McGill," "Rudyard Kipling," "W. B. Yeats" and "Raffles and Miss Blandish." The last-named essay also appeared in the New York monthly magazine, *Politics*. A shortened version of "The Art of Donald McGill" appeared in the *Strand Magazine*. "Arthur Koestler" was written for *Focus*, but will probably not have appeared there before this book is published. "In Defence of P. G. Wodehouse" appeared in the *Windmill*. "Benefit of Clergy" made a sort of phantom appearance in the *Saturday Book* for 1944. The book was in print when its publishers, Messrs. Hutchinsons, decided that this essay must be suppressed on grounds of obscenity. It was accordingly cut out of each copy, though for technical reasons it was impossible to remove its title from the table of contents. To the other periodicals which have allowed me to reprint my contributions, the usual acknowledgments are due.

These essays have been left almost exactly as they were

first written. A few very small changes have been made, mostly corrections of misquotations, and a few footnotes have been added. The latter are dated. The phrase "Great War," when it occurs in the earlier essays, refers to the war of 1914-18. It still seemed great in those days.

G. O.

# CONTENTS

# CHARLES DICKENS

## PART I

DICKENS is one of those writers who are well worth stealing. Even the burial of his body in Westminster Abbey was a species of theft, if you come to think of it.

When Chesterton wrote his introduction to the Everyman Edition of Dickens's works, it seemed quite natural to him to credit Dickens with his own highly individual brand of medievalism, and more recently a Marxist writer, Mr. T. A. Jackson, has made spirited efforts to turn Dickens into a bloodthirsty revolutionary. The Marxist claims him as "almost" a Marxist, the Catholic claims him as "almost" a Catholic, and both claim him as a champion of the proletariat (or "the poor," as Chesterton would have put it). On the other hand, Nadezhda Krupskaya, in her little book on Lenin, relates that towards the end of his life Lenin went to see a dramatized version of *The Cricket on the Hearth*, and found Dickens's "middle-class sentimentality" so intolerable that he walked out in the middle of a scene.

1

Taking "middle class" to mean what Krupskaya might be expected to mean by it, this was probably a truer judgment than those of Chesterton and Jackson. But it is worth noticing that the dislike of Dickens implied in this remark is something unusual. Plenty of people have found him unreadable, but very few seem to have felt any hostility towards the general spirit of his work. Some years ago Mr. Bechhofer Roberts published a full-length attack on Dickens in the form of a novel (*This Side Idolatry*), but it was a merely personal attack, concerned for the most part with Dickens's treatment of his wife. It dealt with incidents which not one in a thousand of Dickens's readers would ever hear about, and which no more invalidate his work than the second-best bed invalidates *Hamlet*. All that the book really demonstrated was that a writer's literary personality has little or nothing to do with his private character. It is quite possible that in private life Dickens was just the kind of insensitive egoist that Mr. Bechhofer Roberts makes him appear. But in his published work there is implied a personality quite different from this, a personality which has won him far more friends than enemies. It might well have been otherwise, for even if Dickens was a bourgeois, he was certainly a subversive writer, a radical, one might truthfully say a rebel. Everyone who has read widely in his work has felt this. Gissing, for instance, the best of the writers on Dickens, was anything but a radical himself, and he disapproved of this strain in Dickens and wished it were not there, but it never occurred to him to deny it. In *Oliver Twist, Hard Times, Bleak House, Little Dorrit,* Dickens attacked English institutions with a ferocity that has never since been approached. Yet he managed to do it without making himself hated, and, more than this, the very people he attacked have swallowed him so completely that he has become a national institution himself. In its attitude towards Dickens the English public has always been a little like the elephant which feels a blow with a walking-stick as a delightful tickling. Before I was ten years old I was having Dickens ladled down my throat by schoolmasters in whom even at that age I could see a strong resemblance to Mr. Creakle, and one knows without needing to be told that lawyers delight in Serjeant Buzfuz and that *Little Dorrit* is a favourite in the Home Office. Dickens seems to have succeeded in attacking everybody and antagonizing nobody. Naturally this makes one wonder whether after all there was something unreal in his attack upon society. Where exactly does he stand, socially, morally and politically? As usual, one can define his position more easily if one starts by deciding what he was *not*.

In the first place he was *not*, as Messrs. Chesterton and Jackson seem to imply, a "proletarian" writer. To begin with, he does not write about the proletariat, in which he merely resembles the overwhelming majority of novelists, past and present. If you look for the working classes in fiction, and especially English fiction, all you find is a hole. This statement needs qualifying, perhaps. For reasons that are easy enough to see, the agricultural labourer (in England a proletarian) gets a fairly good showing in fiction, and a great deal has been written about criminals, derelicts and, more recently, the working-class intelligent-

sia. But the ordinary town proletariat, the people who
make the wheels go round, have always been ignored by
novelists. When they do find their way between the covers
of a book, it is nearly always as objects of pity or as comic
relief. The central action of Dickens's stories almost invariably takes place in middle-class surroundings. If one examines his novels in detail one finds that his real subject-
matter is the London commercial bourgeoisie and their
hangers-on—lawyers, clerks, tradesmen, innkeepers, small
craftsmen and servants. He has no portrait of an agricultural worker, and only one (Stephen Blackpool in *Hard
Times*) of an industrial worker. The Plornishes in *Little
Dorrit* are probably his best picture of a working-class
family—the Peggottys, for instance, hardly belong to the
working class—but on the whole he is not successful with
this type of character. If you ask any ordinary reader
which of Dickens's proletarian characters he can remember, the three he is almost certain to mention are Bill
Sykes, Sam Weller and Mrs. Gamp. A burglar, a valet
and a drunken midwife—not exactly a representative
cross-section of the English working class.

Secondly, in the ordinary accepted sense of the word,
Dickens is not a "revolutionary" writer. But his position
here needs some defining.

Whatever else Dickens may have been, he was not a
hole-and-corner soul-saver, the kind of well-meaning idiot
who thinks that the world will be perfect if you amend a
few by-laws and abolish a few anomalies. It is worth comparing him with Charles Reade, for instance. Reade was a
much better-informed man than Dickens, and in some

ways more public-spirited. He really hated the abuses he could understand, he showed them up in a series of novels which for all their absurdity are extremely readable, and he probably helped to alter public opinion on a few minor but important points. But it was quite beyond him to grasp that, given the existing form of society, certain evils *cannot* be remedied. Fasten upon this or that minor abuse, expose it, drag it into the open, bring it before a British jury, and all will be well—that is how he sees it. Dickens at any rate never imagined that you can cure pimples by cutting them off. In every page of his work one can see a consciousness that society is wrong somewhere at the root. It is when one asks "Which root?" that one begins to grasp his position.

The truth is that Dickens's criticism of society is almost exclusively moral. Hence the utter lack of any constructive suggestion anywhere in his work. He attacks the law, parliamentary government, the educational system and so forth, without ever clearly suggesting what he would put in their places. Of course it is not necessarily the business of a novelist, or a satirist, to make constructive suggestions, but the point is that Dickens's attitude is at bottom not even *de*structive. There is no clear sign that he wants the existing order to be overthrown, or that he believes it would make very much difference if it *were* overthrown. For in reality his target is not so much society as "human nature." It would be difficult to point anywhere in his books to a passage suggesting that the economic system is wrong *as a system*. Nowhere, for instance, does he make any attack on private enterprise or private property.

Even in a book like *Our Mutual Friend*, which turns on the power of corpses to interfere with living people by means of idiotic wills, it does not occur to him to suggest that individuals ought not to have this irresponsible power. Of course one can draw this inference for oneself, and one can draw it again from the remarks about Bounderby's will at the end of *Hard Times*, and indeed from the whole of Dickens's work one can infer the evil of *laissez-faire* capitalism; but Dickens makes no such inference himself. It is said that Macaulay refused to review *Hard Times* because he disapproved of its "sullen Socialism." Obviously Macaulay is here using the word "Socialism" in the same sense in which, twenty years ago, a vegetarian meal or a Cubist picture used to be referred to as "Bolshevism." There is not a line in the book that can properly be called Socialistic; indeed, its tendency if anything is pro-capitalist, because its whole moral is that capitalists ought to be kind, not that workers ought to be rebellious. Bounderby is a bullying windbag and Gradgrind has been morally blinded, but if they were better men, the system would work well enough——that, all through, is the implication. And so far as social criticism goes, one can never extract much more from Dickens than this, unless one deliberately reads meanings into him. His whole "message" is one that at first glance looks like an enormous platitude: If men would behave decently the world would be decent.

Naturally this calls for a few characters who are in positions of authority and who *do* behave decently. Hence that recurrent Dickens figure, the Good Rich Man. This character belongs especially to Dickens's early optimistic period. He is usually a "merchant" (we are not necessarily told what merchandise he deals in), and he is always a superhumanly kind-hearted old gentleman who "trots" to and fro, raising his employees' wages, patting children on the head, getting debtors out of jail and, in general, acting the fairy godmother. Of course he is a pure dream figure, much further from real life than, say, Squeers or Micawber. Even Dickens must have reflected occasionally that anyone who was so anxious to give his money away would never have acquired it in the first place. Mr. Pickwick, for instance, had "been in the city," but it is difficult to imagine him making a fortune there. Nevertheless this character runs like a connecting thread through most of the earlier books. Pickwick, the Cheerybles, old Chuzzlewit, Scrooge—it is the same figure over and over again, the good rich man, handing out guineas. Dickens does however show signs of development here. In the books of the middle period the good rich man fades out to some extent. There is no one who plays this part in *A Tale of Two Cities*, nor in *Great Expectations—Great Expectations* is, in fact, definitely an attack on patronage—and in *Hard Times* it is only very doubtfully played by Gradgrind after his reformation. The character reappears in a rather different form as Meagles in *Little Dorrit* and John Jarndyce in *Bleak House*—one might perhaps add Betsy Trotwood in *David Copperfield*. But in these books the good rich man has dwindled from a "merchant" to a *rentier*. This is significant. A *rentier* is part of the possessing class, he can and, almost without knowing it, does make other people work for him, but he has very little

direct power. Unlike Scrooge or the Cheerybles, he cannot
put everything right by raising everybody's wages. The
seeming inference from the rather despondent books that
Dickens wrote in the 'fifties is that by that time he had
grasped the helplessness of well-meaning individuals in a
corrupt society. Nevertheless, in the last completed novel,
*Our Mutual Friend* (published 1864-65), the good rich
man comes back in full glory in the person of Boffin. Boffin is a proletarian by origin and only rich by inheritance,
but he is the usual *deus ex machina,* solving everybody's
problems by showering money in all directions. He even
"trots," like the Cheerybles. In several ways *Our Mutual
Friend* is a return to the earlier manner, and not an unsuccessful return either. Dickens's thoughts seem to have
come full circle. Once again, individual kindliness is the
remedy for everything.

One crying evil of his time that Dickens says very little
about is child labour. There are plenty of pictures of suffering children in his books, but usually they are suffering
in schools rather than in factories. The one detailed account of child labour that he gives is the description in
*David Copperfield* of little David washing bottles in
Murdstone & Grinby's warehouse. This, of course, is autobiography. Dickens himself, at the age of ten, had worked
in Warren's blacking factory in the Strand, very much as
he describes it here. It was a terribly bitter memory to
him, partly because he felt the whole incident to be discreditable to his parents, and he even concealed it from
his wife till long after they were married. Looking back
on this period, he says in *David Copperfield:*

"It is a matter of some surprise to me, even now, that I can have been so easily thrown away at such an age. A child of excellent abilities and with strong powers of observation, quick, eager, delicate, and soon hurt bodily or mentally, it seems wonderful to me that nobody should have made any sign in my behalf. But none was made; and I became, at ten years old, a little labouring hind in the service of Murdstone & Grinby."

And again, having described the rough boys among whom he worked:

"No words can express the secret agony of my soul as I sunk into this companionship . . . and felt my hopes of growing up to be a learned and distinguished man crushed in my bosom."

Obviously it is not David Copperfield who is speaking, it is Dickens himself. He uses almost the same words on the autobiography that he began and abandoned a few months earlier. Of course Dickens is right in saying that a gifted child ought not to work ten hours a day pasting labels on bottles, but what he does not say is that *no* child ought to be condemned to such a fate, and there is no reason for inferring that he thinks it. David escapes from the warehouse, but Mick Walker and Mealy Potatoes and the others are still there, and there is no sign that this troubles Dickens particularly. As usual, he displays no consciousness that the *structure* of society can be changed. He despises politics, does not believe that any good can come

out of Parliament—he had been a Parliamentary shorthand writer, which was no doubt a disillusioning experience—and he is slightly hostile to the most hopeful movement of his day, trade unionism. In *Hard Times* trade
unionism is represented as something not much better than
a racket, something that happens because employers are
not sufficiently paternal. Stephen Blackpool's refusal to
join the union is rather a virtue in Dickens's eyes. Also,
as Mr. Jackson has pointed out, the apprentices' association in *Barnaby Rudge*, to which Sim Tappertit belongs,
is probably a hit at the illegal or barely legal unions of
Dickens's own day, with their secret assemblies, passwords
and so forth. Obviously he wants the workers to be decently treated, but there is no sign that he wants them to
take their destiny into their own hands, least of all by
open violence.

As it happens, Dickens deals with revolution in the nar-
rower sense in two novels, *Barnaby Rudge* and *A Tale of
Two Cities*. In *Barnaby Rudge* it is a case of rioting
rather than revolution. The Gordon Riots of 1780, though
they had religious bigotry as a pretext, seem to have been
little more than a pointless outburst of looting. Dickens's
attitude to this kind of thing is sufficiently indicated by
the fact that his first idea was to make the ringleaders of
the riots three lunatics escaped from an asylum. He was
dissuaded from this, but the principal figure of the book is
in fact a village idiot. In the chapters dealing with the riots
Dickens shows a most profound horror of mob violence.
He delights in describing scenes in which the "dregs" of
the population behave with atrocious bestiality. These

chapters are of great psychological interest, because they show how deeply he had brooded on this subject. The things he describes can only have come out of his imagination, for no riots on anything like the same scale had happened in his lifetime. Here is one of his descriptions, for instance:

"If Bedlam gates had been flung open wide, there would not have issued forth such maniacs as the frenzy of that night had made. There were men there who danced and trampled on the beds of flowers as though they trod down human enemies, and wrenched them from their stalks, like savages who twisted human necks. There were men who cast their lighted torches in the air, and suffered them to fall upon their heads and faces, blistering the skin with deep unseemly burns. There were men who rushed up to the fire, and paddled in it with their hands as if in water; and others who were restrained by force from plunging in, to gratify their deadly longing. On the skull of one drunken lad—not twenty, by his looks—who lay upon the ground with a bottle to his mouth, the lead from the roof came streaming down in a shower of liquid fire, white hot, melting his head like wax. . . . But of all the howling throng not one learnt mercy from, or sickened at, these sights; nor was the fierce, besotted, senseless rage of one man glutted."

You might almost think you were reading a description of "Red" Spain by a partisan of General Franco. One ought, of course, to remember that when Dickens was

writing, the London "mob" still existed. (Nowadays there
is no mob, only a flock.) Low wages and the growth and
shift of population had brought into existence a huge,
dangerous slum-proletariat, and until the early middle of
the nineteenth century there was hardly such a thing as a
police force. When the brickbats began to fly there was
nothing between shuttering your windows and ordering
the troops to open fire. In *A Tale of Two Cities* he is dealing with a revolution which was really *about* something,
and Dickens's attitude is different, but not entirely different. As a matter of fact, *A Tale of Two Cities* is a book
which tends to leave a false impression behind, especially
after a lapse of time.

The one thing that everyone who has read *A Tale of
Two Cities* remembers is the Reign of Terror. The whole
book is dominated by the guillotine—tumbrils thundering
to and fro, bloody knives, heads bouncing into the basket,
and sinister old women knitting as they watch. Actually
these scenes only occupy a few chapters, but they are
written with terrible intensity, and the rest of the book is
rather slow going. But *A Tale of Two Cities* is not a companion volume to *The Scarlet Pimpernel*. Dickens sees
clearly enough that the French Revolution was bound to
happen and that many of the people who were executed
deserved what they got. If, he says, you behave as the
French aristocracy had behaved, vengeance will follow.
He repeats this over and over again. We are constantly
being reminded that while "my lord" is lolling in bed, with
four liveried footmen serving his chocolate and the peasants starving outside, somewhere in the forest a tree is

growing which will presently be sawn into planks for the platform of the guillotine, etc. etc. etc. The inevitability of the Terror, given its causes, is insisted upon in the clearest terms:

> "It was too much the way . . . to talk of this ter-
> rible Revolution as if it were the only harvest ever
> known under the skies that had not been sown—as if
> nothing had ever been done, or omitted to be done,
> that had led to it—as if observers of the wretched
> millions in France, and of the misused and perverted
> resources that should have made them prosperous,
> had not seen it inevitably coming, years before, and
> had not in plain terms recorded what they saw."

And again:

> "All the devouring and insatiate monsters imag-
> ined since imagination could record itself, are fused
> in the one realisation, Guillotine. And yet there is not
> in France, with its rich variety of soil and climate, a
> blade, a leaf, a root, a sprig, a peppercorn, which
> will grow to maturity under conditions more certain
> than those that have produced this horror. Crush hu-
> manity out of shape once more, under similar ham-
> mers, and it will twist itself into the same tortured
> forms."

In other words, the French aristocracy had dug their own graves. But there is no perception here of what is now called historic necessity. Dickens sees that the results are inevitable, given the causes, but he thinks that the causes

might have been avoided. The Revolution is something
that happens because centuries of oppression have made
the French peasantry sub-human. If the wicked nobleman
could somehow have turned over a new leaf, like Scrooge,
there would have been no Revolution, no *jacquerie*, no
guillotine—and so much the better. This is the opposite
of the "revolutionary" attitude. From the "revolutionary" point of view the class-struggle is the main source of
progress, and therefore the nobleman who robs the peasant and goads him to revolt is playing a necessary part,
just as much as the Jacobin who guillotines the nobleman.
Dickens never writes anywhere a line that can be inter-
preted as meaning this. Revolution as he sees it is merely
a monster that is begotten by tyranny and always ends by
devouring its own instruments. In Sidney Carton's vision
at the foot of the guillotine, he foresees Defarge and the
other leading spirits of the Terror all perishing under the
same knife—which, in fact, was approximately what happened.

And Dickens is very sure that revolution *is* a monster.
That is why everyone remembers the revolutionary scenes
in *A Tale of Two Cities*; they have the quality of nightmare, and it is Dickens's own nightmare. Again and again
he insists upon the meaningless horrors of revolution—the
mass-butcheries, the injustice, the ever-present terror of
spies, the frightful bloodlust of the mob. The descriptions
of the Paris mob—the description, for instance, of the
crowd of murderers struggling round the grindstone to
sharpen their weapons before butchering the prisoners in
the September massacres—outdo anything in *Barnaby*

*Rudge.* The revolutionaries appear to him simply as degraded savages—in fact, as lunatics. He broods over their frenzies with a curious imaginative intensity. He describes them dancing the "Carmagnole," for instance:

> "There could not be fewer than five hundred people, and they were dancing like five thousand demons.
> . . . They danced to the popular Revolution song, keeping a ferocious time that was like a gnashing of teeth in unison. . . . They advanced, retreated, struck at one another's hands, clutched at one another's heads, spun round alone, caught one another, and spun round in pairs, until many of them dropped.
> . . . Suddenly they stopped again, paused, struck out the time afresh, forming into lines the width of the public way, and, with their heads low down and their hands high up, swooped screaming off. No fight could have been half so terrible as this dance. It was so emphatically a fallen sport—a something, once innocent, delivered over to all devilry."

He even credits some of these wretches with a taste for guillotining children. The passage I have abridged above ought to be read in full. It and others like it show how deep was Dickens's horror of revolutionary hysteria. Notice, for instance, that touch, "with their heads low down and their hands high up," etc., and the evil vision it conveys. Madame Defarge is a truly dreadful figure, certainly Dickens's most successful attempt at a *malignant* character. Defarge and others are simply "the new oppressors who have risen on the destruction of the old," the revolutionary courts are presided over by "the lowest, cruellest and worst populace," and so on and so forth. All the way through Dickens insists upon the nightmare insecurity of a revolutionary period, and in this he shows a great deal of prescience. "A law of the suspected, which struck away all security for liberty or life, and delivered over any good and innocent person to any bad and guilty one; prisons gorged with people who had committed no offence, and could obtain no hearing"—it would apply pretty accurately to several countries to-day.

The apologists of any revolution generally try to minimise its horrors; Dickens's impulse is to exaggerate them —and from a historical point of view he has certainly exaggerated. Even the Reign of Terror was a much smaller thing than he makes it appear. Though he quotes no figures, he gives the impression of a frenzied massacre lasting for years, whereas in reality the whole of the Terror, so far as the number of deaths goes, was a joke compared with one of Napoleon's battles. But the bloody knives and the tumbrils rolling to and fro create in his mind a special, sinister vision which he has succeeded in passing on to generations of readers. Thanks to Dickens, the very word "tumbril" has a murderous sound; one forgets that a tumbril is only a sort of farm-cart. To this day, to the average Englishman, the French Revolution means no more than a pyramid of severed heads. It is a strange thing that Dickens, much more in sympathy with the ideas of the Revolution than most Englishmen of his time, should have played a part in creating this impression.

If you hate violence and don't believe in politics, the

only major remedy remaining is education. Perhaps society is past praying for, but there is always hope for the individual human being, if you can catch him young enough. This belief partly accounts for Dickens's preoccupation with childhood.

No one, at any rate no English writer, has written better about childhood than Dickens. In spite of all the knowledge that has accumulated since, in spite of the fact that children are now comparatively sanely treated, no novelist has shown the same power of entering into the child's point of view. I must have been about nine years old when I first read *David Copperfield*. The mental atmosphere of the opening chapters was so immediately intelligible to me that I vaguely imagined they had been written *by a child*. And yet when one re-reads the book as an adult and sees the Murdstones, for instance, dwindle from gigantic figures of doom into semi-comic monsters, these passages lose nothing. Dickens has been able to stand both inside and outside the child's mind, in such a way that the same scene can be wild burlesque or sinister reality, according to the age at which one reads it. Look, for instance, at the scene in which David Copperfield is unjustly suspected of eating the mutton chops; or the scene in which Pip, in *Great Expectations*, coming back from Miss Havisham's house and finding himself completely unable to describe what he has seen, takes refuge in a series of outrageous lies—which, of course, are eagerly believed. All the isolation of childhood is there. And how accurately he has recorded the mechanisms of the child's mind, its visualising tendency, its sensitiveness to certain kinds of impression. Pip relates how in his childhood his ideas about his dead parents were derived from their tombstones:

"The shape of the letters on my father's, gave me an odd idea that he was a square, stout, dark man, with curly black hair. From the character and turn of the inscription, 'ALSO GEORGIANA, WIFE OF THE ABOVE,' I drew a childish conclusion that my mother was freckled and sickly. To five little stone lozenges, each about a foot and a half long, which were arranged in a neat row beside their grave, and were sacred to the memory of five little brothers of mine . . . I am indebted for a belief I religiously entertained that they had all been born on their backs with their hands in their trouser-pockets, and had never taken them out in this state of existence."

There is a similar passage in *David Copperfield*. After biting Mr. Murdstone's hand, David is sent away to school and obliged to wear on his back a placard saying, "Take care of him. He bites." He looks at the door in the playground where the boys have carved their names and from the appearance of each name he seems to know in just what tone of voice the boy will read out the placard:

"There was one boy—a certain J. Steerforth—who cut his name very deep and very often, who, I conceived, would read it in a rather strong voice, and afterwards pull my hair. There was another boy, one Tommy Traddles, who I dreaded would make game of it, and pretend to be dreadfully frightened of me.

There was a third, George Demple, who I fancied would sing it."

When I read this passage as a child, it seemed to me that those were exactly the pictures that those particular names would call up. The reason, of course, is the sound-associations of the words (Demple—"temple"; Traddles —probably "skedaddle"). But how many people, before Dickens, had ever noticed such things? A sympathetic attitude towards children was a much rarer thing in Dickens's day than it is now. The early nineteenth century was not a good time to be a child. In Dickens's youth children were still being "solemnly tried at a criminal bar, where they were held up to be seen," and it was not so long since boys of thirteen had been hanged for petty theft. The doctrine of "breaking the child's spirit" was in full vigour, and *The Fairchild Family* was a standard book for children till late into the century. This evil book is now issued in pretty-pretty expurgated editions, but it is well worth reading in the original version. It gives one some idea of the lengths to which child-discipline was sometimes carried. Mr. Fairchild, for instance, when he catches his children quarreling, first thrashes them, reciting Doctor Watts's "Let dogs delight to bark and bite" between blows of the cane, and then takes them to spend the afternoon beneath a gibbet where the rotting corpse of a murderer is hanging. In the earlier part of the century scores of thousands of children, aged sometimes as young as six, were literally worked to death in the mines or cotton mills, and even at the fashionable public schools boys were flogged till they ran with blood for a mistake in their

Latin verses. One thing which Dickens seems to have recognised, and which most of his contemporaries did not, is the sadistic sexual element in flogging. I think this can be inferred from *David Copperfield* and *Nicholas Nickleby*. But mental cruelty to a child infuriates him as much as physical, and though there is a fair number of exceptions, his schoolmasters are generally scoundrels.

Except for the universities and the big public schools, every kind of education then existing in England gets a mauling at Dickens's hands. There is Doctor Blimber's Academy, where little boys are blown up with Greek until they burst, and the revolting charity schools of the period, which produced specimens like Noah Claypole and Uriah Heep, and Salem House, and Dotheboys Hall, and the disgraceful little dame-school kept by Mr. Wopsle's great-aunt. Some of what Dickens says remains true even to-day. Salem House is the ancestor of the modern "prep. school," which still has a good deal of resemblance to it; and as for Mr. Wopsle's great-aunt, some old fraud of much the same stamp is carrying on at this moment in nearly every small town in England. But, as usual, Dickens's criticism is neither creative nor destructive. He sees the idiocy of an educational system founded on the Greek lexicon and the wax-ended cane; on the other hand, he has no use for the new kind of school that is coming up in the 'fifties and 'sixties, the "modern" school, with its gritty insistence on "facts." What, then, *does* he want? As always, what he appears to want is a moralised version of the existing thing—the old type of school, but with no caning, no bullying or underfeeding, and not quite so much Greek. Doctor Strong's school, to which David Copperfield goes after he escapes from Murdstone & Grinby's, is simply Salem House with the vices left out and a good deal of "old grey stones" atmosphere thrown in:

> "Doctor Strong's was an excellent school, as different from Mr. Creakle's as good is from evil. It was very gravely and decorously ordered, and on a sound system; with an appeal, in everything, to the honour and good faith of the boys . . . which worked wonders. We all felt that we had a part in the management of the place, and in sustaining its character and dignity. Hence, we soon became warmly attached to it—I am sure I did for one, and I never knew, in all my time, of any boy being otherwise—and learnt with a good will, desiring to do it credit. We had noble games out of hours, and plenty of liberty; but even then, as I remember, we were well spoken of in the town, and rarely did any disgrace, by our appearance or manner, to the reputation of Doctor Strong and Doctor Strong's boys."

In the woolly vagueness of this passage one can see Dickens's utter lack of any educational theory. He can imagine the *moral* atmosphere of a good school, but nothing further. The boys "learnt with a good will," but what did they learn? No doubt it was Doctor Blimber's curriculum, a little watered down. Considering the attitude to society that is everywhere implied in Dickens's novels, it comes as rather a shock to learn that he sent his eldest son to Eton and sent all his children through the ordinary

educational mill. Gissing seems to think that he may have
done this because he was painfully conscious of being
under-educated himself. Here perhaps Gissing is influenced by his own love of classical learning. Dickens had
had little or no formal education, but he lost nothing by
missing it, and on the whole he seems to have have been
aware of this. If he was unable to imagine a better school
than Doctor Strong's, or, in real life, than Eton, it was
probably due to an intellectual deficiency rather different
from the one Gissing suggests.

It seems that in every attack Dickens makes upon society he is always pointing to a change of spirit rather
than a change of structure. It is hopeless to try and pin
him down to any definite remedy, still more to any political doctrine. His approach is always along the moral
plane, and his attitude is sufficiently summed up in that
remark about Strong's school being as different from
Creakle's "as good is from evil." Two things can be very
much alike and yet abysmally different. Heaven and Hell
are in the same place. Useless to change institutions without a "change of heart"—that, essentially, is what he is
always saying.

If that were all, he might be no more than a cheer-up
writer, a reactionary humbug. A "change of heart" is in
fact *the* alibi of people who do not wish to endanger the
*status quo*. But Dickens is not a humbug, except in minor
matters, and the strongest single impression one carries
away from his books is that of a hatred of tyranny. I said
earlier that Dickens is not *in the accepted sense* a revolutionary writer. But it is not at all certain that a merely

moral criticism of society may not be just as "revolutionary"—and revolution, after all, means turning things upside down—as the politico-economic criticism which is
fashionable at this moment. Blake was not a politician,
but there is more understanding of the nature of capitalist
society in a poem like "I wander through each charter'd
street" than in three-quarters of Socialist literature.
Progress is not an illusion, it happens, but it is slow and
invariably disappointing. There is always a new tyrant
waiting to take over from the old—generally not quite so
bad, but still a tyrant. Consequently two viewpoints are
always tenable. The one, how can you improve human nature until you have changed the system? The other, what
is the use of changing the system before you have im-
proved human nature? They appeal to different individuals, and they probably show a tendency to alternate in
point of time. The moralist and the revolutionary are constantly undermining one another. Marx exploded a hundred tons of dynamite beneath the moralist position, and
we are still living in the echo of that tremendous crash.
But already, somewhere or other, the sappers are at work
and fresh dynamite is being tamped in place to blow Marx
at the moon. Then Marx, or somebody like him, will come
back with yet more dynamite, and so the process continues,
to an end we cannot yet foresee. The central problem—
how to prevent power from being abused—remains un-
solved. Dickens, who had not the vision to see that private
property is an obstructive nuisance, had the vision to see
that. "If men would behave decently the world would be
decent" is not such a platitude as it sounds.

## PART II

More completely than most writers, perhaps, Dickens can be explained in terms of his social origin, though actually his family history was not quite what one would infer from his novels. His father was a clerk in Government service, and through his mother's family he had connections with both the Army and the Navy. But from the age of nine onwards he was brought up in London in commercial surroundings, and generally in an atmosphere of struggling poverty. Mentally he belongs to the small urban bourgeoisie, and he happens to be an exceptionally fine specimen of this class, with all the "points," as it were, very highly developed. That is partly what makes him so interesting. If one wants a modern equivalent, the nearest would be H. G. Wells, who has had a rather similar history and who obviously owes something to Dickens as a novelist. Arnold Bennett was essentially of the same type, but, unlike the other two, he was a midlander, with an industrial and Nonconformist rather than commercial and Anglican background.

The great disadvantage, and advantage, of the small urban bourgeois is his limited outlook. He sees the world as a middle-class world, and everything outside these limits is either laughable or slightly wicked. On the one hand, he has no contact with industry or the soil; on the other, no contact with the governing classes. Anyone who has studied Wells's novels in detail will have noticed that though he hates the aristocrat like poison, he has no particular

objection to the plutocrat, and no enthusiasm for the proletarian. His most-hated types, the people he believes to be
responsible for all human ills, are kings, landowners,
priests, nationalists, soldiers, scholars and peasants. At
first sight a list beginning with kings and ending with
peasants looks like a mere omnium gatherum, but in reality all these people have a common factor. All of them are
archaic types, people who are governed by tradition and
whose eyes are turned towards the past—the opposite,
therefore, of the rising bourgeois who has put his money
on the future and sees the past simply as a dead hand.

Actually, although Dickens lived in a period when the
bourgeoisie was really a rising class, he displays this characteristic less strongly than Wells. He is almost unconscious of the future and has a rather sloppy love of the
picturesque (the "quaint old church," etc.). Nevertheless
his list of most-hated types is like enough to Wells's for
the similarity to be striking. He is vaguely on the side of
the working class—has a sort of generalised sympathy
with them because they are oppressed—but he does not in
reality know much about them; they come into his books
chiefly as servants, and comic servants at that. At the
other end of the scale he loathes the aristocrat and—going
one better than Wells in this—loathes the big bourgeois
as well. His real sympathies are bounded by Mr. Pickwick
on the upper side and Mr. Barkis on the lower. But the
term "aristocrat," for the type Dickens hates, is vague
and needs defining.

Actually Dickens's target is not so much the great aristocracy, who hardly enter into his books, as their petty

offshoots, the cadging dowagers who live up mews in Mayfair, and the bureaucrats and professional soldiers. All
through his books there are countless hostile sketches of
these people, and hardly any that are friendly. There are
practically no friendly pictures of the landowning class,
for instance. One might make a doubtful exception of Sir
Leicester Dedlock; otherwise there is only Mr. Wardle
(who is a stock figure—the "good old squire") and Hare-
dale in *Barnaby Rudge,* who has Dickens's sympathy because he is a persecuted Catholic. There are no friendly
pictures of soldiers (*i.e.* officers), and none at all of naval
men. As for his bureaucrats, judges and magistrates, most
of them would feel quite at home in the Circumlocution
Office. The only officials whom Dickens handles with any
kind of friendliness are, significantly enough, policemen.

Dickens's attitude is easily intelligible to an Englishman, because it is part of the English puritan tradition,
which is not dead even at this day. The class Dickens belonged to, at least by adoption, was growing suddenly rich
after a couple of centuries of obscurity. It had grown up
mainly in the big towns, out of contact with agriculture,
and politically impotent; government, in its experience,
was something which either interfered or persecuted. Consequently it was a class with no tradition of public service
and not much tradition of usefulness. What now strikes us
as remarkable about the new moneyed class of the nineteenth century is their complete irresponsibility; they see
everything in terms of individual success, with hardly any
consciousness that the community exists. On the other
hand, a Tite Barnacle, even when he was neglecting his

duties, would have some vague notion of what duties he was neglecting. Dickens's attitude is never irresponsible, still less does he take the money-grubbing Smilesian line; but at the back of his mind there is usually a half-belief that the whole apparatus of government is unnecessary. Parliament is simply Lord Coodle and Sir Thomas Doodle, the Empire is simply Major Bagstock and his Indian servant, the Army is simply Colonel Chowser and Doctor Slammer, the public services are simply Bumble and the Circumlocution Office—and so on and so forth. What he does not see, or only intermittently sees, is that Coodle and Doodle and all the other corpses left over from the eighteenth century *are* performing a function which neither Pickwick nor Boffin would ever bother about.

And of course this narrowness of vision is in one way a great advantage to him, because it is fatal for a caricaturist to see too much. From Dickens's point of view "good" society is simply a collection of village idiots. What a crew! Lady Tippins! Mrs. Gowan! Lord Verisopht! The Honourable Bob Stables! Mrs. Sparsit (whose husband was a Powler)! The Tite Barnacles! Nupkins! It is practically a case-book in lunacy. But at the same time his remoteness from the landowning-military-bureaucratic class incapacitates him for full-length satire. He only succeeds with this class when he depicts them as mental defectives. The accusation which used to be made against Dickens in his lifetime, that he "could not paint a gentleman," was an absurdity, but it is true in this sense, that what he says against the "gentleman" class is seldom very damaging. Sir Mulberry Hawk, for instance, is a wretched attempt at the wicked-baronet type. Harthouse in *Hard Times* is better, but he would be only an ordinary achievement for Trollope or Thackeray. Trollope's thoughts hardly move outside the "gentleman" class, but Thackeray has the great advantage of having a foot in two moral camps. In some ways his outlook is very similar to Dickens's. Like Dickens, he identifies with the puritanical moneyed class against the card-playing, debt-bilking aristocracy. The eighteenth century, as he sees it, is sticking out into the nineteenth in the person of the wicked Lord Steyne. *Vanity Fair* is a full-length version of what Dickens did for a few chapters in *Little Dorrit*. But by origins and upbringing Thackeray happens to be somewhat nearer to the class he is satirising. Consequently he can produce such comparatively subtle types as, for instance, Major Pendennis and Rawdon Crawley. Major Pendennis is a shallow old snob, and Rawdon Crawley is a thick-headed ruffian who sees nothing wrong in living for years by swindling tradesmen; but what Thackeray realises is that according to their tortuous code they are neither of them bad men. Major Pendennis would not sign a dud cheque, for instance. Rawdon certainly would, but on the other hand he would not desert a friend in a tight corner. Both of them would behave well on the field of battle—a thing that would not particularly appeal to Dickens. The result is that at the end one is left with a kind of amused tolerance for Major Pendennis and with something approaching respect for Rawdon; and yet one sees, better than any diatribe could make one, the utter rottenness of that kind of cadging, toadying life on the fringes of smart society. Dickens would be quite incapable of this. In his hands both Rawdon and the Major would dwindle to traditional caricatures. And, on the whole, his attacks on "good" society are rather perfunctory. The aristocracy and the big bourgeoisie exist in his books chiefly as a kind of "noises off," a haw-hawing chorus somewhere in the wings, like Podsnap's dinner-parties. When he produces a really subtle and damaging portrait, like John Dorrit or Harold Skimpole, it is generally of some rather middling, unimportant person.

One very striking thing about Dickens, especially considering the time he lived in, is his lack of vulgar nationalism. All peoples who have reached the point of becoming nations tends to despise foreigners, but there is not much doubt that the English-speaking races are the worst offenders. One can see this from the fact that as soon as they become fully aware of any foreign race, they invent an insulting nickname for it. Wop, Dago, Froggy, Squarehead, Kike, Sheeny, Nigger, Wog, Chink, Greaser, Yellowbelly—these are merely a selection. Any time before 1870 the list would have been shorter, because the map of the world was different from what it is now, and there were only three or four foreign races that had fully entered into the English consciousness. But towards these, and especially towards France, the nearest and best-hated nation, the English attitude of patronage was so intolerable that English "arrogance" and "xenophobia" are still a legend. And of course they are not a completely untrue legend even now. Till very recently nearly all English children were brought up to despise the southern European races,

and history as taught in schools was mainly a list of battles won by England. But one has got to read, say, the
*Quarterly Review* of the 'thirties to know what boasting
really is. Those were the days when the English built up
their legend of themselves as "sturdy islanders" and "stub-
born hearts of oak" and when it was accepted as a kind of
scientific fact that one Englishman was the equal of three
foreigners. All through nineteenth-century novels and
comic papers there runs the traditional figure of the
"Froggy"—a small ridiculous man with a tiny beard and
a pointed top-hat, always jabbering and gesticulating,
vain, frivolous and fond of boasting of his martial exploits, but generally taking to flight when real danger
appears. Over against him was John Bull, the "sturdy
English yeoman," or (a more public-school version) the
"strong, silent Englishman" of Charles Kingsley, Tom
Hughes and others.

Thackeray, for instance, has this outlook very strongly,
though there are moments when he sees through it and
laughs at it. The one historical fact that is firmly fixed in
his mind is that the English won the battle of Waterloo.
One never reads far in his books without coming upon
some reference to it. The English, as he sees it, are invincible because of their tremendous physical strength, due
mainly to living on beef. Like most Englishmen of his
time, he has the curious illusion that the English are
larger than other people (Thackeray, as it happened, *was*
larger than most people), and therefore he is capable of
writing passages like this:

"I say to you that you are better than a Frenchman. I would lay even money that you who are reading this are more than five feet seven in height, and
weigh eleven stone; while a Frenchman is five feet
four and does not weigh nine. The Frenchman has
after his soup a dish of vegetables, where you have
one of meat. You are a different and superior animal
—a French-beating animal (the history of hundreds
of years has shown you to be so)," etc. etc.

There are similar passages scattered all through Thackeray's works. Dickens would never be guilty of anything
of the kind. It would be an exaggeration to say that he
nowhere pokes fun at foreigners, and of course, like nearly
all nineteenth-century Englishmen, he is untouched by
European culture. But never anywhere does he indulge in
the typical English boasting, the "island race," "bulldog
breed," "right little, tight little island" style of talk. In
the whole of *A Tale of Two Cities* there is not a line that
could be taken as meaning, "Look how these wicked
Frenchmen behave!" The one place where he seems to display a normal hatred of foreigners is in the American
chapters of *Martin Chuzzlewit*. This, however, is simply
the reaction of a generous mind against cant. If Dickens
were alive to-day he would make a trip to Soviet Russia
and come back with a book rather like Gide's *Retour de
L'URSS*. But he is remarkably free from the idiocy of
regarding nations as individuals. He seldom even makes
jokes turning on nationality. He does not exploit the
comic Irishman and the comic Welshman, for instance,

and not because he objects to stock characters and ready-made jokes, which obviously he does not. It is perhaps more significant that he shows no prejudice against Jews. It is true that he takes it for granted (*Oliver Twist* and *Great Expectations*) that a receiver of stolen goods will be a Jew, which at the time was probably justified. But the "Jew joke," endemic in English literature until the rise of Hitler, does not appear in his books, and in *Our Mutual Friend* he makes a pious though not very convincing attempt to stand up for the Jews.

Dickens's lack of vulgar nationalism is in part the mark of a real largeness of mind, and in part results from his negative, rather unhelpful political attitude. He is very much an Englishman, but he is hardly aware of it—certainly the thought of being an Englishman does not thrill him. He has no imperialist feeling, no discernible views on foreign politics, and is untouched by the military tradition. Temperamentally he is much nearer to the small Nonconformist tradesman who looks down on the "redcoats" and thinks that war is wicked—a one-eyed view, but, after all, war *is* wicked. It is noticeable that Dickens hardly writes of war, even to denounce it. With all his marvellous powers of description, and of describing things he had never seen, he never describes a battle, unless one counts the attack on the Bastille in *A Tale of Two Cities*. Probably the subject would not strike him as interesting, and in any case he would not regard a battlefield as a place where anything worth settling could be settled. It is one up to the lower-middle-class, puritan mentality.

## PART III

Dickens had grown up near enough to poverty to be terrified of it, and in spite of his generosity of mind, he is not
free from the special prejudices of the shabby-genteel. It
is usual to claim him as a "popular" writer, a champion
of the "oppressed masses." So he is, so long as he thinks
of them as oppressed; but there are two things that condi-
tion his attitude. In the first place, he is a south of England man, and a Cockney at that, and therefore out of
touch with the bulk of the real oppressed masses, the industrial and agricultural labourers. It is interesting to see
how Chesterton, another Cockney, always presents Dickens as the spokesman of "the poor," without showing much
awareness of who "the poor" really are. To Chesterton
"the poor" means small shopkeepers and servants. Sam
Weller, he says, "is the great symbol in English literature
of the populace peculiar to England"; and Sam Weller is
a valet! The other point is that Dickens's early experiences have given him a horror of proletarian roughness.
He shows this unmistakably whenever he writes of the very
poorest of the poor, the slum-dwellers. His descriptions of
the London slums are always full of undisguised repul-
sion:

> "The ways were foul and narrow; the shops and
> houses wretched; and people half naked, drunken,
> slipshod and ugly. Alleys and archways, like so many
> cesspools, disgorged their offences of smell, and dirt,
> and life, upon the straggling streets; and the whole

33

quarter reeked with crime, and filth, and misery," etc. etc.

There are many similar passages in Dickens. From them one gets the impression of whole submerged populations whom he regards as being beyond the pale. In rather the same way the modern doctrinaire Socialist contemptuously writes off a large block of the population as "lumpenproletariat." Dickens also shows less understanding of criminals than one would expect of him. Although he is well aware of the social and economic causes of crime, he often seems to feel that when a man has once broken the law he has put himself outside human society. There is a chapter at the end of *David Copperfield* in which David visits the prison where Littimer and Uriah Heep are serving their sentences. Dickens actually seems to regard the horrible "model" prisons, against which Charles Reade delivered his memorable attack in *It is Never too Late to Mend,* as too humane. He complains that the food is too good! As soon as he comes up against crime or the worst depths of poverty, he shows traces of the "I've always kept myself respectable" habit of mind. The attitude of Pip (obviously the attitude of Dickens himself) towards Magwitch in *Great Expectations* is extremely interesting. Pip is conscious all along of his ingratitude towards Joe, but far less so of his ingratitude towards Magwitch. When he discovers that the person who has loaded him with benefits for years is actually a transported convict, he falls into frenzies of disgust. "The abhorrence in which I held the man, the dread I had of him, the repugnance with which I shrank from him, could not have been exceeded if he had been some terrible beast," etc. etc. So far as one can discover from the text, this is not because when Pip was a child he had been terrorised by Magwitch in the churchyard; it is because Magwitch is a criminal and a convict. There is an even more "kept-myself-respectable" touch in the fact that Pip feels as a matter of course that he cannot take Magwitch's money. The money is not the product of a crime, it has been honestly acquired; but it is an ex-convict's money and therefore "tainted." There is nothing psychologically false in this, either. Psychologically the latter part of *Great Expectations* is about the best thing Dickens ever did; throughout this part of the book one feels "Yes, that is just how Pip would have behaved." But the point is that in the matter of Magwitch, Dickens identifies with Pip, and his attitude is at bottom snobbish. The result is that Magwitch belongs to the same queer class of characters as Falstaff and, probably, Don Quixote—characters who are more pathetic than the author intended.

When it is a question of the non-criminal poor, the ordinary, decent, labouring poor, there is of course nothing contemptuous in Dickens's attitude. He has the sincerest admiration for people like the Peggottys and the Plornishes. But it is questionable whether he really regards them as equals. It is of the greatest interest to read Chapter XI of *David Copperfield* and side by side with it the autobiographical fragment (parts of this are given in Forster's *Life*), in which Dickens expresses his feelings about the blacking-factory episode a great deal more strongly than in the novel. For more than twenty years afterwards the memory was so painful to him that he would go out of his way to avoid that part of the Strand. He says that to pass that way "made me cry, after my eldest child could speak." The text makes it quite clear that what hurt him most of all, then and in retrospect, was the enforced contact with "low" associates:

> "No words can express the secret agony of my soul as I sunk into this companionship; compared these everyday associates with those of my happier childhood. . . . But I held some station at the blacking warehouse too. . . . I soon became at least as expeditious and as skilful with my hands as either of the other boys. Though perfectly familiar with them, my conduct and manners were different enough from theirs to place a space between us. They, and the men, always spoke of me as 'the young gentleman.' A certain man . . . used to call me 'Charles' sometimes in speaking to me; but I think it was mostly when we were very confidential. . . . Poll Green uprose once, and rebelled against the 'young-gentleman' usage; but Bob Fagin settled him speedily."

It was as well that there should be "a space between us," you see. However much Dickens may admire the working classes, he does not wish to resemble them. Given his origins, and the time he lived in, it could hardly be otherwise. In the early nineteenth century class-animosities may have been no sharper than they are now, but the surface differences between class and class were enormously greater. The "gentleman" and the "common man" must have seemed like different species of animal. Dickens is quite genuinely on the side of the poor against the rich, but it would be next door to impossible for him not to think of a working-class exterior as a stigma. In one of Tolstoy's fables the peasants of a certain village judge every stranger who arrives from the state of his hands. If his palms are hard from work, they let him in; if his palms are soft, out he goes. This would be hardly intelligible to Dickens; all his heroes have soft hands. His younger heroes—Nicholas Nickleby, Martin Chuzzlewit, Edward Chester, David Copperfield, John Harmon—are usually of the type known as "walking gentlemen." He likes a bourgeois exterior and a bourgeois (not aristocratic) accent. One curious symptom of this is that he will not allow anyone who is to play a heroic part to speak like a working man. A comic hero like Sam Weller, or a merely pathetic figure like Stephen Blackpool, can speak with a broad accent, but the *jeune premier* always speaks the then equivalent of B.B.C. This is so, even when it involves absurdities. Little Pip, for instance, is brought up by people speaking broad Essex, but talks upper-class English from his earliest childhood; actually he would have talked the same dialect as Joe, or at least as Mrs. Gargery. So also with Biddy Wopsle, Lizzie Hexam, Sissie Jupe, Oliver Twist—one ought perhaps to add Little Dorrit. Even Rachel in *Hard Times* has barely a trace of Lancashire accent, an impossibility in her case.

One thing that often gives the clue to a novelist's real feelings on the class question is the attitude he takes up

when class collides with sex. This is a thing too painful to
be lied about, and consequently it is one of the points at
which the "I'm-not-a-snob" pose tends to break down.

One sees that at its most obvious where a class-distinc-
tion is also a colour-distinction. And something resembling
the colonial attitude ("native" women are fair game, white
women are sacrosanct) exists in a veiled form in all-white
communities, causing bitter resentment on both sides.
When this issue arises, novelists often revert to crude
class-feelings which they might disclaim at other times. A
good example of "class-conscious" reaction is a rather forgotten novel, *The People of Clopton*, by Andrew Barton.
The author's moral code is quite clearly mixed up with
class-hatred. He feels the seduction of a poor girl by a rich
man to be something atrocious, a kind of defilement, something quite different from her seduction by a man in her
own walk of life. Trollope deals with this theme twice (*The
Three Clerks* and *The Small House at Allington*) and, as
one might expect, entirely from the upper-class angle. As
he sees it, an affair with a barmaid or a landlady's daughter is simply an "entanglement" to be escaped from. Trollope's moral standards are strict, and he does not allow
the seduction actually to happen, but the implication is
always that a working-class girl's feelings do not greatly
matter. In *The Three Clerks* he even gives the typical
class-reaction by noting that the girl "smells." Meredith
(*Rhoda Fleming*) takes more the "class-conscious" view-
point. Thackeray, as often, seems to hesitate. In *Pendennis* (Fanny Bolton) his attitude is much the same as

Trollope's; in *A Shabby Genteel Story* it is nearer to Meredith's.

One could divine a good deal about Trollope's social origin, or Meredith's, or Barton's, merely from their handling of the class-sex theme. So one can with Dickens, but what emerges, as usual, is that he is more inclined to identify himself with the middle class than with the proletariat. The one incident that seems to contradict this is the tale of the young peasant-girl in Doctor Manette's manuscript in *A Tale of Two Cities*. This, however, is merely a costume-piece put in to explain the implacable hatred of Madame Defarge, which Dickens does not pretend to approve of. In *David Copperfield*, where he is dealing with a typical nineteenth-century seduction, the class-issue does not seem to strike him as paramount. It is a law of Victorian novels that sexual misdeeds must not go unpunished, and so Steerforth is drowned on Yarmouth sands, but neither Dickens, nor old Peggotty, nor even Ham, seems to feel that Steerforth has added to his offence by being the son of rich parents. The Steerforths are moved by class-motives, but the Peggottys are not—not even in the scene between Mrs. Steerforth and old Peggotty; if they were, of course, they would probably turn against David as well as against Steerforth.

In *Our Mutual Friend* Dickens treats the episode of Eugene Wrayburn and Lizzie Hexam very realistically and with no appearance of class bias. According to the "unhand me, monster" tradition, Lizzie ought either to "spurn" Eugene or to be ruined by him and throw herself off Waterloo Bridge; Eugene ought to be either a heart-

less betrayer or a hero resolved upon defying society.
Neither behaves in the least like this. Lizzie is frightened
by Eugene's advances and actually runs away from them,
but hardly pretends to dislike them; Eugene is attracted
by her, has too much decency to attempt seducing her and
dare not marry her because of his family. Finally they are
married and no one is any the worse, except perhaps Mr.
Twemlow, who will lose a few dinner engagements. It is all
very much as it might have happened in real life. But a
"class-conscious" novelist would have given her to Bradley
Headstone.

But when it is the other way about—when it is a case of
a poor man aspiring to some woman who is "above" him—
Dickens instantly retreats into the middle-class attitude.
He is rather fond of the Victorian notion of a woman
(woman with a capital W) being "above" a man. Pip feels
that Estella is "above" him, Esther Summerson is "above"
Guppy, Little Dorrit is "above" John Chivery, Lucy Manette is "above" Sydney Carton. In some of these the
"above"-ness is merely moral, but in others it is social.
There is a scarcely mistakable class-reaction when David
Copperfield discovers that Uriah Heep is plotting to
marry Agnes Wickfield. The disgusting Uriah suddenly
announces that he is in love with her:

> " 'Oh, Master Copperfield, with what a pure affec-
> tion do I love the ground my Agnes walks on.'
> "I believe I had the delirious idea of seizing the
> red-hot poker out of the fire, and running him
> through with it. It went from me with a shock, like a

ball fired from a rifle: but the image of Agnes, out-
raged by so much as a thought of this red-headed
animal's, remained in my mind (when I looked at
him, sitting all awry as if his mean soul griped his
body) and made me giddy. . . . 'I believe Agnes
Wickfield to be as far above *you* [David says later
on], and as far removed from all *your* aspirations, as
that moon herself.' "

Considering how Heep's general lowness—his servile
manners, dropped aitches and so forth—has been rubbed
in throughout the book, there is not much doubt about
the nature of Dickens's feelings. Heep, of course, is playing a villainous part, but even villains have sexual lives;
it is the thought of the "pure" Agnes in bed with a man
who drops his aitches that really revolts Dickens. But his
usual tendency is to treat a man in love with a woman
who is "above" him as a joke. It is one of the stock jokes
of English literature, from Malvolio onwards. Guppy in
*Bleak House* is an example, John Chivery is another, and
there is a rather ill-natured treatment of this theme in the
"swarry" in *Pickwick Papers*. Here Dickens describes the
Bath footmen as living a kind of fantasy-life, holding dinner-parties in imitation of their "betters" and deluding
themselves that their young mistresses are in love with
them. This evidently strikes him as very comic. So it is, in
a way, though one might question whether it is not better
for a footman even to have delusions of this kind than
simply to accept his status in the spirit of the catechism.

In his attitude towards servants Dickens is not ahead of

his age. In the nineteenth century the revolt against domestic service was just beginning, to the great annoyance
of everyone with over £500 a year. An enormous number
of the jokes in nineteenth-century comic papers deal with
the uppishness of servants. For years *Punch* ran a series
of jokes called "Servant Gal-isms," all turning on the then
astonishing fact that a servant is a human being. Dickens
is sometimes guilty of this kind of thing himself. His books
abound with the ordinary comic servants; they are dishonest (*Great Expectations*), incompetent (*David Copperfield*), turn up their noses at good food (*Pickwick
Papers*), etc. etc.— all rather in the spirit of the subur-
ban housewife with one downtrodden cook-general. But
what is curious, in a nineteenth-century radical, is that
when he wants to draw a sympathetic picture of a servant,
he creates what is recognisably a feudal type. Sam Weller,
Mark Tapley, Clara Peggotty are all of them feudal figures. They belong to the *genre* of the "old family re-
tainer"; they identify themselves with their master's
family and are at once doggishly faithful and completely
familiar. No doubt Mark Tapley and Sam Weller are
derived to some extent from Smollett, and hence from
Cervantes; but it is interesting that Dickens should have
been attracted by such a type. Sam Weller's attitude is
definitely medieval. He gets himself arrested in order to
follow Mr. Pickwick into the Fleet, and afterwards refuses
to get married because he feels that Mr. Pickwick still
needs his services. There is a characteristic scene between
them:

" 'Vages or no vages, board or no board, lodgin' or no lodgin', Sam Veller, as you took from the old inn in the Borough, sticks by you, come what may. . . .'

" 'My good fellow,' said Mr. Pickwick, when Mr. Weller had sat down again, rather abashed at his own enthusiasm, 'you are bound to consider the young woman also.'

" 'I do consider the young 'ooman, sir,' said Sam. 'I have considered the young 'ooman. I've spoke to her. I've told her how I'm sitivated; she's ready to vait till I'm ready, and I believe she vill. If she don't, she's not the young 'ooman I take her for, and I give her up with readiness.' "

It is easy to imagine what the young woman would have said to this in real life. But notice the feudal atmosphere. Sam Weller is ready as a matter of course to sacrifice years of life to his master, and he can also sit down in his master's presence. A modern manservant would never think of doing either. Dickens's views on the servant question do not get much beyond wishing that master and servant would love one another. Sloppy in *Our Mutual Friend*, though a wretched failure as a character, represents the same kind of loyalty as Sam Weller. Such loyalty, of course, is natural, human and likeable; but so was feudalism.

What Dickens seems to be doing, as usual, is reaching out for an idealised version of the existing thing. He was writing at a time when domestic service must have seemed a completely inevitable evil. There were no labour-saving devices, and there was huge inequality of wealth. It was an age of enormous families, pretentious meals and inconvenient houses, when the slavey drudging fourteen hours a day in the basement kitchen was something too normal to be noticed. And given the *fact* of servitude, the feudal relationship is the only tolerable one. Sam Weller and Mark Tapley are dream figures, no less than the Cheerybles. If there have got to be masters and servants, how much better that the master should be Mr. Pickwick and the servant should be Sam Weller. Better still, of course, if servants did not exist at all—but this Dickens is probably unable to imagine. Without a high level of mechanical development, human equality is not practically possible; Dickens goes to show that it is not imaginable either.

**PART IV**

It is not merely a coincidence that Dickens never writes about agriculture and writes endlessly about food. He was a Cockney, and London is the centre of the earth in rather the same sense that the belly is the centre of the body. It is a city of consumers, of people who are deeply civilised but not primarily useful. A thing that strikes one when one looks below the surface of Dickens's books is that, as nineteenth-century novelists go, he is rather ignorant. He knows very little about the way things really happen. At first sight this statement looks flatly untrue, and it needs some qualification.

Dickens had had vivid glimpses of "low life"—life in a debtor's prison, for example—and he was also a popular novelist and able to write about ordinary people. So were all the characteristic English novelists of the nineteenth century. They felt at home in the world they lived in, whereas a writer nowadays is so hopelessly isolated that the typical modern novel is a novel about a novelist. Even when Joyce, for instance, spends a decade or so in patient efforts to make contact with the "common man," his "common man" finally turns out to be a Jew, and a bit of a highbrow at that. Dickens at least does not suffer from this kind of thing. He has no difficulty in introducing the common motives, love, ambition, avarice, vengeance and so forth. What he does not noticeably write about, however, is *work*.

In Dickens's novels anything in the nature of work happens off-stage. The only one of his heroes who has a plausible profession is David Copperfield, who is first a shorthand writer and then a novelist, like Dickens himself. With most of the others, the way they earn their living is very much in the background. Pip, for instance, "goes into business" in Egypt; we are not told what business, and Pip's working life occupies about half a page of the book. Clennam has been in some unspecified business in China, and later goes into another barely specified business with Doyce. Martin Chuzzlewit is an architect, but does not seem to get much time for practising. In no case do their adventures spring directly out of their work. Here the contrast between Dickens and, say, Trollope is startling. And one reason for this is undoubtedly that

Dickens knows very little about the professions his characters are supposed to follow. What exactly went on in Gradgrind's factories? How did Podsnap make his money? How did Merdle work his swindles? One knows that Dickens could never follow up the details of Parliamentary elections and Stock Exchange rackets as Trollope could. As soon as he has to deal with trade, finance, industry or politics he takes refuge in vagueness, or in satire. This is the case even with legal processes, about which actually he must have known a good deal. Compare any lawsuit in Dickens with the lawsuit in *Orley Farm*, for instance.

And this partly accounts for the needless ramifications of Dickens's novels, the awful Victorian "plot." It is true that not all his novels are alike in this. *A Tale of Two Cities* is a very good and fairly simple story, and so in its different way is *Hard Times*; but these are just the two which are always rejected as "not like Dickens"—and incidentally they were not published in monthly numbers.[1] The two first-person novels are also good stories, apart from their sub-plots. But the typical Dickens novel, *Nicholas Nickleby, Oliver Twist, Martin Chuzzlewit, Our Mutual Friend*, always exists round a framework of melodrama. The last thing anyone ever remembers about these books is their central story. On the other hand, I suppose

[1] *Hard Times* was published as a serial in *Household Words* and *Great Expectations* and *A Tale of Two Cities* in *All the Year Round*. Forster says that the shortness of the weekly instalments made it "much more difficult to get sufficient interest into each." Dickens himself complained of the lack of "elbow-room." In other words, he had to stick more closely to the story.

no one has ever read them without carrying the memory of individual pages to the day of his death. Dickens sees human beings with the most intense vividness, but he sees them always in private life, as "characters," not as functional members of society; that is to say, he sees them statically. Consequently his greatest success is *The Pickwick Papers*, which is not a story at all, merely a series of sketches; there is little attempt at development—the characters simply go on and on, behaving like idiots, in a kind of eternity. As soon as he tries to bring his characters into action, the melodrama begins. He cannot make the action revolve round their ordinary occupations; hence the crossword puzzle of coincidences, intrigues, murders, disguises, buried wills, long-lost brothers, etc. etc. In the end even people like Squeers and Micawber get sucked into the machinery.

Of course it would be absurd to say that Dickens is a vague or merely melodramatic writer. Much that he wrote is extremely factual, and in the power of evoking visual images he has probably never been equalled. When Dickens has once described something you see it for the rest of your life. But in a way the concreteness of his vision is a sign of what he is missing. For, after all, that is what the merely casual onlooker always sees—the outward appearance, the non-functional, the surfaces of things. No one who is really involved in the landscape ever sees the landscape. Wonderfully as he can describe an *appearance*, Dickens does not often describe a *process*. The vivid pictures that he succeeds in leaving in one's memory are nearly always the pictures of things seen in leisure mo-

ments, in the coffee-rooms of country inns or through the
windows of a stage-coach; the kind of things he notices are
inn-signs, brass door-knockers, painted jugs, the interiors
of shops and private houses, clothes, faces and, above all,
food. Everything is seen from the consumer-angle. When
he writes about Coketown he manages to evoke, in just a
few paragraphs, the atmosphere of a Lancashire town as
a slightly disgusted southern visitor would see it. "It had a
black canal in it, and a river that ran purple with evil-
smelling dye, and vast piles of buildings full of windows
where there was a rattling and a trembling all day long,
and where the piston of the steam-engine worked monot-
onously up and down, like the head of an elephant in a
state of melancholy madness." That is as near as Dickens
ever gets to the machinery of the mills. An engineer or a
cotton-broker would see it differently; but then neither of
them would be capable of that impressionistic touch about
the heads of the elephants.

In a rather different sense his attitude to life is extremely unphysical. He is a man who lives through his eyes
and ears rather than through his hands and muscles. Actually his habits were not so sedentary as this seems to
imply. In spite of rather poor health and physique, he was
active to the point of restlessness; throughout his life he
was a remarkable walker, and he could at any rate car-
penter well enough to put up stage scenery. But he was
not one of those people who feel a need to use their hands.
It is difficult to imagine him digging at a cabbage-patch,
for instance. He gives no evidence of knowing anything
about agriculture, and obviously knows nothing about any

kind of game or sport. He has no interest in pugilism, for
instance. Considering the age in which he was writing, it is
astonishing how little physical brutality there is in Dickens's novels. Martin Chuzzlewit and Mark Tapley, for instance, behave with the most remarkable mildness towards
the Americans who are constantly menacing them with revolvers and bowie-knives. The average English or American novelist would have had them handing out socks on
the jaw and exchanging pistol-shots in all directions.
Dickens is too decent for that; he sees the stupidity of
violence, and also he belongs to a cautious urban class
which does not deal in socks on the jaw, even in theory.
And his attitude towards sport is mixed up with social
feelings. In England, for mainly geographical reasons,
sport, especially field-sports, and snobbery are inextrica-
bly mingled. English Socialists are often flatly incredulous
when told that Lenin, for instance, was devoted to shooting. In their eyes shooting, hunting, etc., are simply snobbish observances of the landed gentry; they forget that
these things might appear differently in a huge virgin
country like Russia. From Dickens's point of view almost
any kind of sport is at best a subject for satire. Consequently one side of nineteenth-century life—the boxing,
racing, cockfighting, badger-digging, poaching, rat-catch-
ing side of life, so wonderfully embalmed in Leech's illustrations to Surtees—is outside his scope.

What is more striking, in a seemingly "progressive"
radical, is that he is not mechanically minded. He shows
no interest either in the details of machinery or in the
things machinery can do. As Gissing remarks, Dickens no-

where describes a railway journey with anything like the
enthusiasm he shows in describing journeys by stage-
coach. In nearly all of his books one has a curious feeling
that one is living in the first quarter of the nineteenth
century, and in fact, he does tend to return to this period.
*Little Dorrit*, written in the middle 'fifties, deals with the
late 'twenties; *Great Expectations* (1861) is not dated,
but evidently deals with the 'twenties and 'thirties. Several
of the inventions and discoveries which have made the
modern world possible (the electric telegraph, the breech-
loading gun, india-rubber, coal gas, wood-pulp paper)
first appeared in Dickens's lifetime, but he scarcely notes
them in his books. Nothing is queerer than the vagueness
with which he speaks of Doyce's "invention" in *Little Dorrit*. It is represented as something extremely ingenious and
revolutionary, "of great importance to his country and
his fellow-creatures," and it is also an important minor
link in the book; yet we are never told what the "invention" is! On the other hand, Doyce's physical appearance
is hit off with the typical Dickens touch; he has a peculiar
way of moving his thumb, a way characteristic of engineers. After that, Doyce is firmly anchored in one's memory; but, as usual, Dickens has done it by fastening on
something external.

There are people (Tennyson is an example) who lack
the mechanical faculty but can see the social possibilities
of machinery. Dickens has not this stamp of mind. He
shows very little consciousness of the future. When he
speaks of human progress it is usually in terms of *moral*
progress—men growing better; probably he would never

admit that men are only as good as their technical development allows them to be. At this point the gap between Dickens and his modern analogue, H. G. Wells, is at its widest. Wells wears the future round his neck like a millstone, but Dickens's unscientific cast of mind is just as damaging in a different way. What it does is to make any *positive* attitude more difficult for him. He is hostile to the feudal, agricultural past and not in real touch with the industrial present. Well, then, all that remains is the future (meaning Science, "progress" and so forth), which hardly enters into his thoughts. Therefore, while attacking everything in sight, he has no definable standard of comparison. As I have pointed out already, he attacks the current educational system with perfect justice, and yet, after all, he has no remedy to offer except kindlier schoolmasters. Why did he not indicate what a school *might* have been? Why did he not have his own sons educated according to some plan of his own, instead of sending them to public schools to be stuffed with Greek? Because he lacked that kind of imagination. He has an infallible moral sense, but very little intellectual curiosity. And here one comes upon something which really is an enormous deficiency in Dickens, something that really does make the nineteenth century seem remote from us—that he has no ideal of *work*.

With the doubtful exception of David Copperfield (merely Dickens himself), one cannot point to a single one of his central characters who is primarily interested in his job. His heroes work in order to make a living and to marry the heroine, not because they feel a passionate in-

terest in one particular subject. Martin Chuzzlewit, for
instance, is not burning with zeal to be an architect; he
might just as well be a doctor or a barrister. In any case,
in the typical Dickens novel, the *deus ex machina* enters
with a bag of gold in the last chapter and the hero is ab-
solved from further struggle. The feeling, "This is what
I came into the world to do. Everything else is uninteresting. I will do this even if it means starvation," which turns
men of differing temperaments into scientists, inventors,
artists, priests, explorers and revolutionaries—this motif
is almost entirely absent from Dickens's books. He himself, as is well known, worked like a slave and believed in
his work as few novelists have ever done. But there seems
to be no calling except novel-writing (and perhaps acting) towards which he can imagine this kind of devotion.
And, after all, it is natural enough, considering his rather
negative attitude towards society. In the last resort there
is nothing he admires except common decency. Science is
uninteresting and machinery is cruel and ugly (the heads
of the elephants). Business is only for ruffians like Bounderby. As for politics—leave that to the Tite Barnacles.
Really there is no objective except to marry the heroine,
settle down, live solvently and be kind. And you can do
that much better in private life.

Here, perhaps, one gets a glimpse of Dickens's secret
imaginative background. What did he think of as the most
desirable way to live? When Martin Chuzzlewit had made
it up with his uncle, when Nicholas Nickleby had married
money, when John Harmon had been enriched by Boffin—
what did they *do?*

The answer evidently is that they did nothing. Nicholas Nickleby invested his wife's money with the Cheerybles and "became a rich and prosperous merchant," but as he immediately retired into Devonshire, we can assume that he did not work very hard. Mr. and Mrs. Snodgrass "purchased and cultivated a small farm, more for occupation than profit." That is the spirit in which most of Dickens's books end—a sort of radiant idleness. Where he appears to disapprove of young men who do not work (Harthouse, Harry Gowan, Richard Carstone, Wrayburn before his reformation), it is because they are cynical and immoral or because they are a burden on somebody else; if you are "good," and also self-supporting, there is no reason why you should not spend fifty years in simply drawing your dividends. Home life is always enough. And, after all, it was the general assumption of his age. The "genteel sufficiency," the "competence," the "gentleman of independent means" (or "in easy circumstances")—the very phrases tell one all about the strange, empty dream of the eighteenth- and nineteenth-century middle bourgeoisie. It was a dream of *complete idleness*. Charles Reade conveys its spirit perfectly in the ending of *Hard Cash*. Alfred Hardie, hero of *Hard Cash*, is the typical nineteenth-century novel-hero (public-school style), with gifts which Reade describes as amounting to "genius." He is an old Etonian and a scholar of Oxford, he knows most of the Greek and Latin classics by heart, he can box with prize-fighters and win the Diamond Sculls at Henley. He goes through incredible adventures in which, of course, he behaves with faultless heroism, and then, at the age of

twenty-five, he inherits a fortune, marries his Julia Dodd
and settles down in the suburbs of Liverpool, in the same
house as his parents-in-law:

> "They all lived together at Albion Villa, thanks to
> Alfred. . . . Oh, you happy little villa! You were as
> like Paradise as any mortal dwelling can be. A day
> came, however, when your walls could no longer hold
> all the happy inmates. Julia presented Alfred with a
> lovely boy; enter two nurses and the villa showed
> symptoms of bursting. Two months more, and Alfred
> and his wife overflowed into the next villa. It was but
> twenty yards off; and there was a double reason for
> the migration. As often happens after a long separa-
> tion, Heaven bestowed on Captain and Mrs. Dodd
> another infant to play about their knees," etc. etc. etc.

This is the type of the Victorian happy ending—a
vision of a huge, loving family of three or four generations, all crammed together in the same house and constantly multiplying, like a bed of oysters. What is striking
about it is the utterly soft, sheltered, effortless life that it
implies. It is not even a violent idleness, like Squire
Western's. That is the significance of Dickens's urban
background and his non-interest in the blackguardly-
sporting-military side of life. His heroes, once they had
come into money and "settled down," would not only do no
work; they would not even ride, hunt, shoot, fight duels,
elope with actresses or lose money at the races. They
would simply live at home in feather-bed respectability,

and preferably next door to a blood-relation living exactly
the same life:

> "The first act of Nicholas, when he became a rich
> and prosperous merchant, was to buy his father's old
> house. As time crept on, and there came gradually
> about him a group of lovely children, it was altered
> and enlarged; but none of the old rooms were ever
> pulled down, no old tree was ever rooted up, nothing
> with which there was any association of bygone times
> was ever removed or changed.
>
> "Within a stone's-throw was another retreat en-
> livened by children's pleasant voices too; and here
> was Kate ... the same true, gentle creature, the same
> fond sister, the same in the love of all about her, as
> in her girlish days."

It is the same incestuous atmosphere as in the passage
quoted from Reade. And evidently this is Dickens's ideal
ending. It is perfectly attained in *Nicholas Nickleby,
Martin Chuzzlewit* and *Pickwick,* and it is approximated
to in varying degrees in almost all the others. The exceptions are *Hard Times* and *Great Expectations*—the latter
actually has a "happy ending," but it contradicts the general tendency of the book, and it was put in at the request
of Bulwer Lytton.

The ideal to be striven after, then, appears to be something like this: a hundred thousand pounds, a quaint old
house with plenty of ivy on it, a sweetly womanly wife, a
horde of children, and no work. Everything is safe, soft,
peaceful and, above all, domestic. In the moss-grown

churchyard down the road are the graves of the loved ones who passed away before the happy ending happened. The servants are comic and feudal, the children prattle round your feet, the old friends sit at your fireside, talking of past days, there is the endless succession of enormous meals, the cold punch and sherry negus, the feather beds and warming-pans, the Christmas parties with charades and blind man's buff; but nothing ever happens, except the yearly childbirth. The curious thing is that it is a genuinely happy picture, or so Dickens is able to make it appear. The thought of that kind of existence is satisfying to him. This alone would be enough to tell one that more than a hundred years have passed since Dickens's first book was written. No modern man could combine such purposelessness with so much vitality.

## PART V

By this time anyone who is a lover of Dickens, and who has read as far as this, will probably be angry with me.

I have been discussing Dickens simply in terms of his "message," and almost ignoring his literary qualities. But every writer, especially every novelist, *has* a "message," whether he admits it or not, and the minutest details of his work are influenced by it. All art is propaganda. Neither Dickens himself nor the majority of Victorian novelists would have thought of denying this. On the other hand, not all propaganda is art. As I said earlier, Dickens is one of those writers who are felt to be worth stealing. He has been stolen by Marxists, by Catholics and, above all, by Conservatives. The question is, What is there to steal? Why does anyone care about Dickens? Why do *I* care about Dickens?

That kind of question is never easy to answer. As a rule, an æsthetic preference is either something inexplicable or it is so corrupted by non-æsthetic motives as to make one wonder whether the whole of literary criticism is not a huge network of humbug. In Dickens's case the complicating factor is his familiarity. He happens to be one of those "great authors" who are ladled down everyone's throat in childhood. At the time this causes rebellion and vomiting, but it may have different after-effects in later life. For instance, nearly everyone feels a sneaking affection for the patriotic poems that he learned by heart as a child, "Ye Mariners of England," the "Charge of the Light Brigade" and so forth. What one enjoys is not so much the poems themselves as the memories they call up. And with Dickens the same forces of association are at work. Probably there are copies of one or two of his books lying about in an actual majority of English homes. Many children begin to know his characters by sight before they can even read, for on the whole Dickens was lucky in his illustrators. A thing that is absorbed as early as that does not come up against any critical judgment. And when one thinks of this, one thinks of all that is bad and silly in Dickens—the cast-iron "plots," the characters who don't come off, the *longueurs*, the paragraphs in blank verse, the awful pages of "pathos." And then the thought arises,

when I say I like Dickens, do I simply mean that I like
thinking about my childhood? Is Dickens merely an institution?

If so, he is an institution that there is no getting away
from. How often one really thinks about any writer, even
a writer one cares for, is a difficult thing to decide; but I
should doubt whether anyone who has actually read Dickens can go a week without remembering him in one context
or another. Whether you approve of him or not, he is
*there*, like the Nelson Column. At any moment some scene
or character, which may come from some book you cannot
even remember the name of, is liable to drop into your
mind. Micawber's letters! Winkle in the witness-box! Mrs.
Gamp! Mrs. Wititterly and Sir Tumley Snuffim! Todgers's! (George Gissing said that when he passed the
Monument it was never of the Fire of London that he
thought, always of Todgers's). Mrs. Leo Hunter!
Squeers! Silas Wegg and the Decline and Fall-off of the
Russian Empire! Miss Mills and the Desert of Sahara!
Wopsle acting Hamlet! Mrs. Jellyby! Mantalini, Jerry
Cruncher, Barkis, Pumblechook, Tracy Tupman, Skimpole, Joe Gargery, Pecksniff—and so it goes on and on.
It is not so much a series of books, it is more like a world.
And not a purely comic world either, for part of what one
remembers in Dickens is his Victorian morbidness and
necrophilia and the blood-and-thunder scenes—the death
of Sykes, Krook's spontaneous combustion, Fagin in the
condemned cell, the women knitting round the guillotine.
To a surprising extent all this has entered even into the
minds of people who do not care about it. A music-hall

comedian can (or at any rate could quite recently) go on
the stage and impersonate Micawber or Mrs. Gamp with a
fair certainty of being understood, although not one in
twenty of the audience had ever read a book of Dickens's
right through. Even people who affect to despise him
quote him unconsciously.

Dickens is a writer who can be imitated, up to a certain
point. In genuinely popular literature—for instance, the
Elephant and Castle version of *Sweeny Todd*—he has
been plagiarised quite shamelessly. What has been imitated, however, is simply a tradition that Dickens himself
took from earlier novelists and developed, the cult of
"character," *i.e.*, eccentricity. The thing that cannot be
imitated is his fertility of invention, which is invention not
so much of characters, still less of "situations," as of turns
of phrase and concrete details. The outstanding, unmistakable mark of Dickens's writing is the *unnecessary detail*. Here is an example of what I mean. The story given
below is not particularly funny, but there is one phrase in
it that is as individual as a fingerprint. Mr. Jack Hopkins,
at Bob Sawyer's party, is telling the story of the child who
swallowed its sister's necklace:

> "Next day, child swallowed two beads; the day
> after that, he treated himself to three, and so on, till
> in a week's time he had got through the necklace—
> five-and-twenty beads in all. The sister, who was an
> industrious girl and seldom treated herself to a bit of
> finery, cried her eyes out at the loss of the necklace;
> looked high and low for it; but I needn't say, didn't

find it. A few days afterwards, the family were at dinner—baked shoulder of mutton and potatoes under it—the child, who wasn't hungry, was playing about the room, when suddenly there was heard the devil of a noise, like a small hailstorm. 'Don't do that, my boy,' says the father. 'I ain't a-doin' nothing,' said the child. 'Well, don't do it again,' said the father. There was a short silence, and then the noise began again, worse than ever. 'If you don't mind what I say, my boy,' said the father, 'you'll find yourself in bed, in something less than a pig's whisper.' He gave the child a shake to make him obedient, and such a rattling ensued as nobody ever heard before. 'Why, dam' me, it's *in* the child,' said the father; 'he's got the croup in the wrong place!' 'No, I haven't, father,' said the child, beginning to cry, 'it's the necklace; I swallowed it, father.' The father caught the child up, and ran with him to the hospital, the beads in the boy's stomach rattling all the way with the jolting; and the people looking up in the air, and down in the cellars, to see where the unusual sound came from. 'He's in the hospital now,' said Jack Hopkins, 'and he makes such a devil of a noise when he walks about, that they're obliged to muffle him in a watchman's coat, for fear he should wake the patients.' "

As a whole, this story might come out of any nineteenth-century comic paper. But the unmistakable Dickens touch, the thing nobody else would have thought of, is the baked shoulder of mutton and potatoes under it. How does this advance the story? The answer is that it doesn't. It is something totally unnecessary, a florid little squiggle on the edge of the page; only, it is by just these squiggles that the special Dickens atmosphere is created. The other thing one would notice here is that Dickens's way of telling a story takes a long time. An interesting example, too long to quote, is Sam Weller's story of the obstinate patient in Chapter XLIV of *The Pickwick Papers*. As it happens, we have a standard of comparison here, because Dickens is plagiarising, consciously or unconsciously. The story is also told by some ancient Greek writer. I cannot now find the passage, but I read it years ago as a boy at school, and it runs more or less like this:

"A certain Thracian, renowned for his obstinacy, was warned by his physician that if he drank a flagon of wine it would kill him. The Thracian thereupon drank the flagon of wine and immediately jumped off the house-top and perished. 'For,' said he, 'in this way I shall prove that the wine did not kill me.'"

As the Greek tells it, that is the whole story—about six lines. As Sam Weller tells it, it takes round about a thousand words. Long before getting to the point we have been told all about the patient's clothes, his meals, his manners, even the newspapers he reads, and about the peculiar construction of the doctor's carriage, which conceals the fact that the coachman's trousers do not match his coat. Then there is the dialogue between the doctor and the patient. "'Crumpets is wholesome, sir,' said the patient. 'Crum-

pets is *not* wholesome, sir,' says the doctor, wery fierce,"
etc. etc. In the end the original story has been buried
under the details. And in all of Dickens's most characteristic passages it is the same. His imagination overwhelms
everything, like a kind of weed. Squeers stands up to ad-
dress his boys, and immediately we are hearing about
Bolder's father who was two pounds ten short, and Mobbs's
stepmother who took to her bed on hearing that Mobbs
wouldn't eat fat and hoped Mr. Squeers would flog him
into a happier state of mind. Mrs. Leo Hunter writes a
poem, "Expiring Frog"; two full stanzas are given. Boffin
takes a fancy to pose as a miser, and instantly we are
down among the squalid biographies of eighteenth-cen-
tury misers, with names like Vulture Hopkins and the
Rev. Blewberry Jones, and chapter headings like "The
Story of the Mutton Pies" and "The Treasures of a
Dunghill." Mrs. Harris, who does not even exist, has more
detail piled on to her than any three characters in an ordinary novel. Merely in the middle of a sentence we learn,
for instance, that her infant nephew has been seen in a
bottle at Greenwich Fair, along with the pink-eyed lady,
the Prussian dwarf and the living skeleton. Joe Gargery
describes how the robbers broke into the house of Pumblechook, the corn and seed merchant—"and they took his
till, and they took his cash box, and they drinked his wine,
and they partook of his wittles, and they slapped his face,
and they pulled his nose, and they tied him up to his bed-
pust, and they give him a dozen, and they stuffed his
mouth full of flowering annuals to perwent his crying
out." Once again the unmistakable Dickens touch, the

flowering annuals; but any other novelist would only have mentioned about half of these outrages. Everything is piled up and up, detail on detail, embroidery on embroidery. It is futile to object that this kind of thing is rococo —one might as well make the same objection to a wedding-cake. Either you like it or you do not like it. Other nineteenth-century writers, Surtees, Barham, Thackeray, even Marryat, have something of Dickens's profuse, overflowing quality, but none of them on anything like the same scale. The appeal of all these writers now depends partly on period-flavour, and though Marryat is still officially a "boys' writer" and Surtees has a sort of legendary fame among hunting men, it is probable that they are read mostly by bookish people.

Significantly, Dickens's most successful books (not his *best* books) are *The Pickwick Papers*, which is not a novel, and *Hard Times* and *A Tale of Two Cities*, which are not funny. As a novelist his natural fertility greatly hampers him, because the burlesque which he is never able to resist is constantly breaking into what ought to be serious situations. There is a good example of this in the opening chapter of *Great Expectations*. The escaped convict, Magwitch, has just captured the six-year-old Pip in the churchyard. The scene starts terrifyingly enough, from Pip's point of view. The convict, smothered in mud and with his chain trailing from his leg, suddenly starts up among the tombs, grabs the child, turns him upside down and robs his pockets. Then he begins terrorising him into bringing food and a file:

"He held me by the arms in an upright position on the top of the stone, and went on in these fearful terms:

" 'You bring me, to-morrow morning early, that file and them wittles. You bring the lot to me, at that old Battery over yonder. You do it, and you never dare to say a word or dare to make a sign concerning your having seen such a person as me, or any person sumever, and you shall be let to live. You fail, or you go from my words in any partickler, no matter how small it is, and your heart and liver shall be tore out, roasted and ate. Now, I ain't alone, as you may think I am. There's a young man hid with me, in comparison with which young man I am a Angel. That young man hears the words I speak. That young man has a secret way pecooliar to himself, of getting at a boy, and at his heart, and at his liver. It is in wain for a boy to attempt to hide himself from that young man. A boy may lock his door, may be warm in bed, may tuck himself up, may draw the clothes over his head, may think himself comfortable and safe, but that young man will softly creep and creep his way to him and tear him open. I am keeping that young man from harming you at the present moment, but with great difficulty. I find it wery hard to hold that young man off of your inside. Now, what do you say?' "

Here Dickens has simply yielded to temptation. To begin with, no starving and hunted man would speak in the least like that. Moreover, although the speech shows a remarkable knowledge of the way in which a child's mind works, its actual words are quite out of tune with what is to follow. It turns Magwitch into a sort of pantomime wicked uncle, or, if one sees him through the child's eyes, into an appalling monster. Later in the book he is to be represented as neither, and his exaggerated gratitude, on which the plot turns, is to be incredible because of just this speech. As usual, Dickens's imagination has overwhelmed him. The picturesque details were too good to be left out. Even with characters who are more of a piece than Magwitch he is liable to be tripped up by some seductive phrase. Mr. Murdstone, for instance, is in the habit of ending David Copperfield's lessons every morning with a dreadful sum in arithmetic. "If I go into a cheesemonger's shop, and buy five thousand double-Gloucester cheeses at fourpence halfpenny each, present payment," it always begins. Once again the typical Dickens detail, the double-Gloucester cheeses. But it is far too human a touch for Murdstone; he would have made it five thousand cash-boxes. Every time this note is struck, the unity of the novel suffers. Not that it matters very much, because Dickens is obviously a writer whose parts are greater than his wholes. He is all fragments, all details—rotten architecture, but wonderful gargoyles—and never better than when he is building up some character who will later on be forced to act inconsistently.

Of course it is not usual to urge against Dickens that he makes his characters behave inconsistently. Generally he is accused of doing just the opposite. His characters are supposed to be mere "types," each crudely representing some single trait and fitted with a kind of label by which you recognise him. Dickens is "only a caricaturist"—that is the usual accusation, and it does him both more and less than justice. To begin with, he did not think of himself as a caricaturist, and was constantly setting into action characters who ought to have been purely static. Squeers, Micawber, Miss Mowcher,[1] Wegg, Skimpole, Pecksniff and many others are finally involved in "plots" where they are out of place and where they behave quite incredibly. They start off as magic-lantern slides and they end by getting mixed up in a third-rate movie. Sometimes one can put one's finger on a single sentence in which the original illusion is destroyed. There is such a sentence in *David Copperfield*. After the famous dinner-party (the one where the leg of mutton was underdone), David is showing his guests out. He stops Traddles at the top of the stairs:

> " 'Traddles,' said I, 'Mr. Micawber don't mean any harm, poor fellow: but if I were you I wouldn't lend him anything.'
>
> " 'My dear Copperfield,' returned Traddles smiling, 'I haven't got anything to lend.'
>
> " 'You have got a name, you know,' I said."

At the place where one reads it this remark jars a little,

[1] Dickens turned Miss Mowcher into a sort of heroine because the real woman whom he had caricatured had read the earlier chapters and was bitterly hurt. He had previously meant her to play a villainous part. But *any* action by such a character would seem incongruous.

though something of the kind was inevitable sooner or later. The story is a fairly realistic one, and David is growing up; ultimately he is bound to see Mr. Micawber for what he is, a cadging scoundrel. Afterwards, of course, Dickens's sentimentality overcomes him and Micawber is made to turn over a new leaf. But from then on, the original Micawber is never quite recaptured, in spite of desperate efforts. As a rule, the "plot" in which Dickens's characters get entangled is not particularly credible, but at least it makes some pretence at reality, whereas the world to which they belong is a never-never land, a kind of eternity. But just here one sees that "only a caricaturist" is not really a condemnation. The fact that Dickens is always thought of as a caricaturist, although he was constantly trying to be something else, is perhaps the surest mark of his genius. The monstrosities that he created are still remembered as monstrosities, in spite of getting mixed up in would-be probable melodramas. Their first impact is so vivid that nothing that comes afterwards effaces it. As with the people one knew in childhood, one seems always to remember them in one particular attitude, doing one particular thing. Mrs. Squeers is always ladling out brimstone and treacle, Mrs. Gummidge is always weeping, Mrs. Gargery is always banging her husband's head against the wall, Mrs. Jellyby is always scribbling tracts while her children fall into the area—and there they all are, fixed for ever like little twinkling miniatures painted on snuffbox lids, completely fantastic and incredible, and yet somehow more solid and infinitely more memorable than the efforts of serious novelists. Even by the standards of his time Dickens was an exceptionally artificial writer. As Ruskin said, he "chose to work in a circle of stage fire." His characters are even more distorted and simplified than Smollett's. But there are no rules in novel-writing, and for any work of art there is only one test worth bothering about—survival. By this test Dickens's characters have succeeded, even if the people who remember them hardly think of them as human beings. They are monsters, but at any rate they *exist*.

But all the same there is a disadvantage in writing about monsters. It amounts to this, that it is only certain moods that Dickens can speak to. There are large areas of the human mind that he never touches. There is no poetic feeling anywhere in his books, and no genuine tragedy, and even sexual love is almost outside his scope. Actually his books are not so sexless as they are sometimes declared to be, and considering the time in which he was writing, he is reasonably frank. But there is not a trace in him of the feeling that one finds in *Manon Lescaut, Salâmmbo, Carmen, Wuthering Heights*. According to Aldous Huxley, D. H. Lawrence once said that Balzac was "a gigantic dwarf," and in a sense the same is true of Dickens. There are whole worlds which he either knows nothing about or does not wish to mention. Except in a rather roundabout way, one cannot *learn* very much from Dickens. And to say this is to think almost immediately of the great Russian novelists of the nineteenth century. Why is it that Tolstoy's grasp seems to be so much larger than Dickens's —why is it that he seems able to tell you so much more *about yourself?* It is not that he is more gifted, or even, in the last analysis, more intelligent. It is because he is writing about people who are growing. His characters are struggling to make their souls, whereas Dickens's are already finished and perfect. In my own mind Dickens's people are present far more often and far more vividly than Tolstoy's, but always in a single unchangeable attitude, like pictures or pieces of furniture. You cannot hold an imaginary conversation with a Dickens character as you can with, say, Pierre Bezoukhov. And this is not merely because of Tolstoy's greater seriousness, for there are also comic characters that you can imagine yourself talking to —Bloom, for instance, or Pécuchet, or even Wells's Mr. Polly. It is because Dickens's characters have no mental life. They say perfectly the thing that they have to say, but they cannot be conceived as talking about anything else. They never learn, never speculate. Perhaps the most meditative of his characters is Paul Dombey, and his thoughts are mush. Does this mean that Tolstoy's novels are "better" than Dickens's? The truth is that it is absurd to make such comparisons in terms of "better" and "worse." If I were forced to compare Tolstoy with Dickens, I should say that Tolstoy's appeal will probably be wider in the long run, because Dickens is scarcely intelligible outside the English-speaking culture; on the other hand, Dickens is able to reach simple people, which Tolstoy is not. Tolstoy's characters can cross a frontier, Dickens's can be portrayed on a cigarette-card. But one is no more obliged to choose between them than between a sausage and a rose. Their purposes barely intersect.

## PART VI

If Dickens had been *merely* a comic writer, the chances are that no one would now remember his name. Or at best a few of his books would survive in rather the same way as books like *Frank Fairleigh, Mr. Verdant Green* and *Mrs. Caudle's Curtain Lectures*, as a sort of hangover of the Victorian atmosphere, a pleasant little whiff of oysters and brown stout. Who has not felt sometimes that it was "a pity" that Dickens ever deserted the vein of *Pickwick* for things like *Little Dorrit* and *Hard Times?* What people always demand of a popular novelist is that he shall write the same book over and over again, forgetting that a man who would write the same book twice could not even write it once. Any writer who is not utterly lifeless moves upon a kind of parabola, and the downward curve is implied in the upward one. Joyce has to start with the frigid competence of *Dubliners* and end with the dream-language of *Finnegan's Wake*, but *Ulysses* and *Portrait of the Artist* are part of the trajectory. The thing that drove Dickens forward into a form of art for which he was not really suited, and at the same time caused us to remember him, was simply the fact that he was a moralist, the consciousness of his "having something to say." He is always preaching a sermon, and that is the final secret of his inventiveness. For you can only create if you can *care*. Types like Squeers and Micawber could not have been produced by a hack writer looking for something to be funny about. A joke worth laughing at always has an idea behind it, and

usually a subversive idea. Dickens is able to go on being
funny because he is in revolt against authority, and authority is always there to be laughed at. There is always
room for one more custard pie.

His radicalism is of the vaguest kind, and yet one always knows that it is there. That is the difference between
being a moralist and a politician. He has no constructive
suggestions, not even a clear grasp of the nature of the
society he is attacking, only an emotional perception that
something is wrong. All he can finally say is, "Behave
decently," which, as I suggested earlier, is not necessarily
so shallow as it sounds. Most revolutionaries are potential
Tories, because they imagine that everything can be put
right by altering the *shape* of society; once that change is
effected, as it sometimes is, they see no need for any other.
Dickens has not this kind of mental coarseness. The vagueness of his discontent is the mark of its permanence. What
he is out against is not this or that institution, but, as
Chesterton put it, "an expression on the human face."
Roughly speaking, his morality is the Christian morality,
but in spite of his Anglican upbringing he was essentially
a Bible-Christian, as he took care to make plain when writing his will. In any case he cannot properly be described
as a religious man. He "believed," undoubtedly, but religion in the devotional sense does not seem to have entered
much into his thoughts.[1] Where he is Christian is in his

---

[1] From a letter to his youngest son (in 1868): "You will remember that you have never at home been harassed about religious observances, or mere formalities. I have always been anxious not to weary my children with such things, before they are

quasi-instinctive siding with the oppressed against the oppressors. As a matter of course he is on the side of the underdog, always and everywhere. To carry this to its logical conclusion one has got to change sides when the underdog becomes an upperdog, and in fact Dickens does tend to do so. He loathes the Catholic Church, for instance, but as soon as the Catholics are persecuted (*Barnaby Rudge*) he is on their side. He loathes the aristocratic class even more, but as soon as they are really overthrown (the revolutionary chapters in *A Tale of Two Cities*) his sympathies swing round. Whenever he departs from this emotional attitude he goes astray. A well-known example is at the ending of *David Copperfield*, in which everyone who reads it feels that something has gone wrong. What is wrong is that the closing chapters are pervaded, faintly but noticeably, by the cult of success. It is the gospel according to Smiles, instead of the gospel according to Dickens. The attractive, out-at-elbow characters are got rid of, Micawber makes a fortune, Heep gets into prison—both of these events are flagrantly impossible—and even Dora is killed off to make way for Agnes. If you like, you can read Dora as Dickens's wife and Agnes as his sister-in-law, but the essential point is that Dickens has "turned respec-

old enough to form opinions respecting them. You will therefore understand the better that I now most solemnly impress upon you the truth and beauty of the Christian Religion, as it came from Christ Himself, and the impossibility of your going far wrong if you humbly but heartily respect it. . . . Never abandon the wholesome practice of saying your own private prayers, night and morning. I have never abandoned it myself, and I know the comfort of it."

table" and done violence to his own nature. Perhaps that is why Agnes is the most disagreeable of his heroines, the real legless angel of Victorian romance, almost as bad as Thackeray's Laura.

No grown-up person can read Dickens without feeling his limitations, and yet there does remain his native generosity of mind, which acts as a kind of anchor and nearly always keeps him where he belongs. It is probably the central secret of his popularity. A good-tempered antinomianism rather of Dickens's type is one of the marks of Western popular culture. One sees it in folk-stories and comic songs, in dream-figures like Mickey Mouse and Pop-eye the Sailor (both of them variants of Jack the Giant-killer), in the history of working-class Socialism, in the popular protests (always ineffective but not always a sham) against imperialism, in the impulse that makes a jury award excessive damages when a rich man's car runs over a poor man; it is the feeling that one is always on the side of the underdog, on the side of the weak against the strong. In one sense it is a feeling that is fifty years out of date. The common man is still living in the mental world of Dickens, but nearly every modern intellectual has gone over to some or other form of totalitarianism. From the Marxist or Fascist point of view, nearly all that Dickens stands for can be written off as "bourgeois morality." But in moral outlook no one could be more "bourgeois" than the English working classes. The ordinary people in the Western countries have never entered, mentally, into the world of "realism" and power-politics. They may do so before long, in which case Dickens will be as out of date as the cab-horse. But in his own age and ours he has been popular chiefly because he was able to express in a comic, simplified and therefore memorable form the native decency of the common man. And it is important that from this point of view people of very different types can be described as "common." In a country like England, in spite of its class-structure, there does exist a certain cultural unity. All through the Christian ages, and especially since the French Revolution, the Western world has been haunted by the idea of freedom and equality; it is only an *idea*, but it has penetrated to all ranks of society. The most atrocious injustices, cruelties, lies, snobberies exist everywhere, but there are not many people who can regard these things with the same indifference as, say, a Roman slave-owner. Even the millionaire suffers from a vague sense of guilt, like a dog eating a stolen leg of mutton. Nearly everyone, whatever his actual conduct may be, responds emotionally to the idea of human brotherhood. Dickens voiced a code which was and on the whole still is believed in, even by people who violate it. It is difficult otherwise to explain why he could be both read by working people (a thing that has happened to no other novelist of his stature) and buried in Westminster Abbey.

When one reads any strongly individual piece of writing, one has the impression of seeing a face somewhere behind the page. It is not necessarily the actual face of the writer. I feel this very strongly with Swift, with Defoe, with Fielding, Stendhal, Thackeray, Flaubert, though in several cases I do not know what these people looked like and do not want to know. What one sees is the face that the writer *ought* to have. Well, in the case of Dickens I see a face that is not quite the face of Dickens's photographs, though it resembles it. It is the face of a man of about forty, with a small beard and a high colour. He is laughing, with a touch of anger in his laughter, but no triumph, no malignity. It is the face of a man who is always fighting against something, but who fights in the open and is not frightened, the face of a man who is *generously angry*—in other words, of a nineteenth-century liberal, a free intelligence, a type hated with equal hatred by all the smelly little orthodoxies which are now contending for our souls.

**1939**

# BOYS' WEEKLIES

YOU never walk far through any poor quarter in any big town without coming upon a small newsagent's shop. The general appearance of these shops is always very much the same: a few posters for the *Daily Mail* and the *News of the World* outside, a poky little window with sweet-bottles and packets of Players, and a dark interior smelling of liquorice allsorts and festooned from floor to ceiling with vilely printed twopenny papers, most of them with lurid cover-illustrations in three colours.

Except for the daily and evening papers, the stock of these shops hardly overlaps at all with that of the big newsagents. Their main selling line is the twopenny weekly, and the number and variety of these are almost unbelievable. Every hobby and pastime—cage-birds, fretwork, carpentering, bees, carrier-pigeons, home conjuring, philately, chess—has at least one paper devoted to it, and generally several. Gardening and livestock-keeping must have at least a score between them. Then there are the sporting papers, the radio papers, the children's comics, the various snippet papers such as *Tit-bits*, the large

range of papers devoted to the movies and all more or less
exploiting women's legs, the various trade papers, the
women's story-papers (the *Oracle, Secrets, Peg's Paper,*
etc. etc.), the needlework papers—these so numerous that
a display of them alone will often fill an entire window—
and in addition the long series of "Yank Mags" (*Fight
Stories, Action Stories, Western Short Stories,* etc.),
which are imported shop-soiled from America and sold at
twopence halfpenny or threepence. And the periodical
proper shades off into the fourpenny novelette, the *Aldine
Boxing Novels,* the *Boys' Friend Library,* the *Schoolgirls'
Own Library* and many others.

Probably the contents of these shops is the best avail-
able indication of what the mass of the English people
really feels and thinks. Certainly nothing half so revealing exists in documentary form. Best-seller novels, for instance, tell one a great deal, but the novel is aimed almost
exclusively at people above the £4-a-week level. The movies
are probably a very unsafe guide to popular taste, because
the film industry is virtually a monopoly, which means that
it is not obliged to study its public at all closely. The same
applies to some extent to the daily papers, and most of all
to the radio. But it does not apply to the weekly paper
with a smallish circulation and specialised subject-matter.
Papers like the *Exchange and Mart,* for instance, or
*Cage-Birds,* or the *Oracle,* or *Prediction,* or the *Matri-
monial Times,* only exist because there is a definite demand
for them, and they reflect the minds of their readers as a
great national daily with a circulation of millions cannot
possibly do.

Here I am only dealing with a single series of papers, the boys' twopenny weeklies, often inaccurately described as "penny dreadfuls." Falling strictly within this class there are at present ten papers, the *Gem, Magnet, Modern Boy, Triumph* and *Champion,* all owned by the Amalgamated Press, and the *Wizard, Rover, Skipper, Hotspur* and *Adventure,* all owned by D. C. Thomson & Co. What the circulations of these papers are, I do not know. The editors and proprietors refuse to name any figures, and in any case the circulation of a paper carrying serial stories is bound to fluctuate widely. But there is no question that the combined public of the ten papers is a very large one. They are on sale in every town in England, and nearly every boy who reads at all goes through a phase of reading one or more of them. The *Gem* and *Magnet,* which are much the oldest of these papers, are of rather different type from the rest, and they have evidently lost some of their popularity during the past few years. A good many boys now regard them as old-fashioned and "slow." Nevertheless I want to discuss them first, because they are more interesting psychologically than the others, and also because the mere survival of such papers into the nineteen-thirties is a rather startling phenomenon.

The *Gem* and *Magnet* are sister-papers (characters out of one paper frequently appear in the other), and were both started more than thirty years ago. At that time, together with *Chums* and the old *B.O.P.,* they were the leading papers for boys, and they remained dominant till quite recently. Each of them carries every week a fifteen- or twenty-thousand-word school story, complete in itself, but usually more or less connected with the story of the week before. The *Gem* in addition to its school story carries one or more adventure serials. Otherwise the two papers are so much alike that they can be treated as one, though the *Magnet* has always been the better known of the two, probably because it possesses a really first-rate character in the fat boy, Billy Bunter.

The stories are stories of what purports to be public-school life, and the schools (Greyfriars in the *Magnet* and St. Jim's in the *Gem*) are represented as ancient and fashionable foundations of the type of Eton or Winchester. All the leading characters are fourth-form boys aged fourteen or fifteen, older or younger boys only appearing in very minor parts. Like Sexton Blake and Nelson Lee, these boys continue week after week and year after year, never growing any older. Very occasionally a new boy arrives or a minor character drops out, but in at any rate the last twenty-five years the personnel has barely altered. All the principal characters in both papers—Bob Cherry, Tom Merry, Harry Wharton, Johnny Bull, Billy Bunter and the rest of them—were at Greyfriars or St. Jim's long before the Great War, exactly the same age as at present, having much the same kind of adventures and talking almost exactly the same dialect. And not only the characters but the whole atmosphere of both *Gem* and *Magnet* has been preserved unchanged, partly by means of very elaborate stylisation. The stories in the *Magnet* are signed "Frank Richards" and those in the *Gem*, "Martin Clifford," but a series lasting thirty years could hardly be the

work of the same person every week.[1] Consequently they
have to be written in a style that is easily imitated—an
extraordinary, artificial, repetitive style, quite different
from anything else now existing in English literature. A
couple of extracts will do as illustrations. Here is one from
the *Magnet*:

"Groan!

"'Shut up, Bunter!'

"Groan!

"Shutting up was not really in Billy Bunter's line.
He seldom shut up, though often requested to do so.
On the present awful occasion the fat Owl of Greyfriars was less inclined than ever to shut up. And he
did not shut up! He groaned, and groaned, and went
on groaning.

"Even groaning did not fully express Bunter's
feelings. His feelings, in fact, were inexpressible.

"There were six of them in the soup! Only one of
the six uttered sounds of woe and lamentation. But
that one, William George Bunter, uttered enough for
the whole party and a little over.

"Harry Wharton & Co. stood in a wrathy and wor-
ried group. They were landed and stranded, diddled,
dished and done!" etc. etc. etc.

[1] 1945. This is quite incorrect. These stories have been written
throughout the whole period by "Frank Richards" and "Martin
Clifford," who are one and the same person! See articles in *Horizon*, May 1940, and *Summer Pie*, summer 1944.

Here is one from the *Gem*:

" 'Oh cwumbs!'
" 'Oh gum!'
" 'Oooogh!'
" 'Urrggh!'

"Arthur Augustus sat up dizzily. He grabbed his handkerchief and pressed it to his damaged nose. Tom Merry sat up, gasping for breath. They looked at one another.

" 'Bai Jove! This is a go, deah boy!' gurgled Arthur Augustus. 'I have been thrown into quite a fluttah! Oogh! The wottahs! The wuffians! The feahful outsidahs! Wow!' " etc. etc. etc.

Both of these extracts are entirely typical; you would find something like them in almost every chapter of every number, to-day or twenty-five years ago. The first thing that anyone would notice is the extraordinary amount of tautology (the first of these two passages contains a hundred and twenty-five words and could be compressed into about thirty), seemingly designed to spin out the story, but actually playing its part in creating the atmosphere. For the same reason various facetious expressions are repeated over and over again; "wrathy," for instance, is a great favourite, and so is "diddled, dished and done." "Oooogh!", "Grooo!" and "Yaroo!" (stylised cries of pain) recur constantly, and so does "Ha! ha! ha!", always given a line to itself, so that sometimes a quarter of a column or thereabouts consists of "Ha! ha! ha!" The slang

("Go and eat coke!", "What the thump!", "You frabjous ass!", etc. etc.) has never been altered, so that the boys are now using slang which is at least thirty years out of date. In addition, the various nicknames are rubbed in on every possible occasion. Every few lines we are reminded that Harry Wharton & Co. are "the Famous Five," Bunter is always "the fat Owl" or "the Owl of the Remove," Vernon-Smith is always "the Bounder of Greyfriars," Gussy (the Honourable Arthur Augustus D'Arcy) is always "the swell of St. Jim's," and so on and so forth. There is a constant, untiring effort to keep the atmosphere intact and to make sure that every new reader learns immediately who is who. The result has been to make Greyfriars and St. Jim's into an extraordinary little world of their own, a world which cannot be taken seriously by anyone over fifteen, but which at any rate is not easily forgotten. By a debasement of the Dickens technique a series of stereotyped "characters" has been built up, in several cases very successfully. Billy Bunter, for instance, must be one of the best-known figures in English fiction; for the mere number of people who know him he ranks with Sexton Blake, Tarzan, Sherlock Holmes and a handful of characters in Dickens.

Needless to say, these stories are fantastically unlike life at a real public school. They run in cycles of rather differing types, but in general they are the clean-fun, knockabout type of story, with interest centring round horseplay, practical jokes, ragging masters, fights, canings, football, cricket and food. A constantly recurring story is one in which a boy is accused of some misdeed committed

by another and is too much of a sportsman to reveal the
truth. The "good" boys are "good" in the clean-living
Englishman tradition—they keep in hard training, wash
behind their ears, never hit below the belt, etc. etc.—and
by way of contrast there is a series of "bad" boys, Racke,
Crooke, Loder and others, whose badness consists in bet-
ting, smoking cigarettes and frequenting public-houses.
All these boys are constantly on the verge of expulsion,
but as it would mean a change of personnel if any boy
were actually expelled, no one is ever caught out in any
really serious offence. Stealing, for instance, barely enters
as a motif. Sex is completely taboo, especially in the form
in which it actually arises at public schools. Occasionally
girls enter into the stories, and very rarely there is something approaching a mild flirtation, but it is always entirely in the spirit of clean fun. A boy and a girl enjoy
going for bicycle rides together—that is all it ever
amounts to. Kissing, for instance, would be regarded as
"soppy." Even the bad boys are presumed to be completely sexless. When the *Gem* and *Magnet* were started,
it is probable that there was a deliberate intention to get
away from the guilty sex-ridden atmosphere that pervaded so much of the earlier literature for boys. In the
'nineties the *Boys' Own Paper*, for instance, used to have
its correspondence columns full of terrifying warnings
against masturbation, and books like *St. Winifred's* and
*Tom Brown's Schooldays* were heavy with homosexual
feeling, though no doubt the authors were not fully aware
of it. In the *Gem* and *Magnet* sex simply does not exist as
a problem. Religion is also taboo; in the whole thirty

years' issue of the two papers the word "God" probably does not occur, except in "God save the King." On the other hand, there has always been a very strong "temperance" strain. Drinking and, by association, smoking are regarded as rather disgraceful even in an adult ("shady" is the usual word), but at the same time as something irresistibly fascinating, a sort of substitute for sex. In their moral atmosphere the *Gem* and *Magnet* have a great deal in common with the Boy Scout movement, which started at about the same time.

All literature of this kind is partly plagiarism. Sexton Blake, for instance, started off quite frankly as an imitation of Sherlock Holmes, and still resembles him fairly strongly; he has hawklike features, lives in Baker Street, smokes enormously and puts on a dressing-gown when he wants to think. The *Gem* and *Magnet* probably owe something to the school-story writers who were flourishing when they began, Gunby Hadath, Desmond Coke and the rest, but they owe more to nineteenth-century models. In so far as Greyfriars and St. Jim's are like real schools at all, they are much more like Tom Brown's Rugby than a modern public school. Neither school has an O.T.C., for instance, games are not compulsory, and the boys are even allowed to wear what clothes they like. But without doubt the main origin of these papers is *Stalky & Co*. This book has had an immense influence on boys' literature, and it is one of those books which have a sort of traditional reputation among people who have never even seen a copy of it. More than once in boys' weekly papers I have come across a reference to *Stalky & Co*. in which the word was spelt

"Storky." Even the name of the chief comic among the Greyfriars masters, Mr. Prout, is taken from *Stalky & Co.*, and so is much of the slang; "jape," "merry," "giddy," "bizney" (business), "frabjous," "don't" for "doesn't"—all of them out of date even when *Gem* and *Magnet* started. There are also traces of earlier origins. The name "Greyfriars" is probably taken from Thackeray, and Gosling, the school porter in the *Magnet*, talks in an imitation of Dickens's dialect.

With all this, the supposed "glamour" of public-school life is played for all it is worth. There is all the usual paraphernalia—lock-up, roll-call, house matches, fagging, prefects, cosy teas round the study fire, etc. etc.—and constant reference to the "old school," the "old grey stones" (both schools were founded in the early sixteenth century), the "team spirit" of the "Greyfriars men." As for the snob-appeal, it is completely shameless. Each school has a titled boy or two whose titles are constantly thrust in the reader's face; other boys have the names of well-known aristocratic families, Talbot, Manners, Lowther. We are for ever being reminded that Gussy is the Honourable Arthur A. D'Arcy, son of Lord Eastwood, that Jack Blake is heir to "broad acres," that Hurree Jamset Ram Singh (nicknamed Inky) is the Nabob of Bhanipur, that Vernon-Smith's father is a millionaire. Till recently the illustrations in both papers always depicted the boys in clothes imitated from those of Eton; in the last few years Greyfriars has changed over to blazers and flannel trousers, but St. Jim's still sticks to the Eton jacket, and Gussy sticks to his top-hat. In the school magazine which ap-

pears every week as part of the *Magnet*, Harry Wharton
writes an article discussing the pocket-money received by
the "fellows in the Remove," and reveals that some of them
get as much as five pounds a week! This kind of thing is a
perfectly deliberate incitement to wealth-fantasy. And
here it is worth noticing a rather curious fact, and that is
that the school story is a thing peculiar to England. So
far as I know, there are extremely few school stories in
foreign languages. The reason, obviously, is that in England education is mainly a matter of status. The most definite dividing-line between the petite-bourgeoisie and the
working class is that the former pay for their education,
and within the bourgeoisie there is another unbridgeable
gulf between the "public" school and the "private" school.
It is quite clear that there are tens and scores of thousands
of people to whom every detail of life at a "posh" public
school is wildly thrilling and romantic. They happen to be
outside that mystic world of quadrangles and house-col-
ours, but they yearn after it, day-dream about it, live
mentally in it for hours at a stretch. The question is, Who
are these people? Who reads the *Gem* and *Magnet?*

Obviously one can never be quite certain about this
kind of thing. All I can say from my own observation is
this. Boys who are likely to go to public schools themselves
generally read the *Gem* and *Magnet*, but they nearly always stop reading them when they are about twelve; they
may continue for another year from force of habit, but by
that time they have ceased to take them seriously. On the
other hand, the boys at very cheap private schools, the
schools that are designed for people who can't afford a

public school but consider the Council schools "common,"
continue reading the *Gem* and *Magnet* for several years
longer. A few years ago I was a teacher at two of these
schools myself. I found that not only did virtually all the
boys read the *Gem* and *Magnet*, but that they were still
taking them fairly seriously when they were fifteen or even
sixteen. These boys were the sons of shopkeepers, office
employees and small business and professional men, and
obviously it is this class that the *Gem* and *Magnet* are
aimed at. But they are certainly read by working-class
boys as well. They are generally on sale in the poorest
quarters of big towns, and I have known them to be read
by boys whom one might expect to be completely immune
from public-school "glamour." I have seen a young coal-
miner, for instance, a lad who had already worked a year
or two underground, eagerly reading the *Gem*. Recently I
offered a batch of English papers to some British legionaries of the French Foreign Legion in North Africa; they
picked out the *Gem* and *Magnet* first. Both papers are
much read by girls,[1] and the Pen Pals department of the
*Gem* shows that it is read in every corner of the British
Empire, by Australians, Canadians, Palestine Jews, Ma-
lays, Arabs, Straits Chinese, etc. etc. The editors evidently
expect their readers to be aged around about fourteen, and
the advertisements (milk chocolate, postage stamps, water
pistols, blushing cured, home conjuring tricks, itching

---

[1] There are several corresponding girls' papers. The *Schoolgirl*
is companion-paper to the *Magnet* and has stories by "Hilda
Richards." The characters are interchangeable to some extent.
Bessie Bunter, Billy Bunter's sister, figures in the *Schoolgirl*.

powder, the Phine Phun Ring which runs a needle into your friend's hand, etc. etc.) indicate roughly the same age; there are also the Admiralty advertisements, however, which call for youths between seventeen and twenty-two. And there is no question that these papers are also read by adults. It is quite common for people to write to the editor and say that they have read every number of the *Gem* or *Magnet* for the past thirty years. Here, for instance, is a letter from a lady in Salisbury:

"I can say of your splendid yarns of Harry Wharton & Co., of Greyfriars, that they never fail to reach a high standard. Without doubt they are the finest stories of their type on the market to-day, which is saying a good deal. They seem to bring you face to face with Nature. I have taken the *Magnet* from the start, and have followed the adventures of Harry Wharton & Co. with rapt interest. I have no sons, but two daughters, and there's always a rush to be the first to read the grand old paper. My husband, too, was a staunch reader of the *Magnet* until he was suddenly taken away from us."

It is well worth getting hold of some copies of the *Gem* and *Magnet*, especially the *Gem*, simply to have a look at the correspondence columns. What is truly startling is the intense interest with which the pettiest details of life at Greyfriars and St. Jim's are followed up. Here, for instance, are a few of the questions sent in by readers:

"What age is Dick Roylance?" "How old is St. Jim's?" "Can you give me a list of the Shell and their

studies?" "How much did D'Arcy's monocle cost?"
"How is it fellows like Crooke are in the Shell and
decent fellows like yourself are only in the Fourth?"
"What are the Form captain's three chief duties?"
"Who is the chemistry master at St. Jim's?" (From
a girl) "Where is St. Jim's situated? *Could* you tell
me how to get there, as I would love to see the building? Are you boys just 'phoneys,' as I think you
are?"

It is clear that many of the boys and girls who write
these letters are living a complete fantasy-life. Sometimes
a boy will write, for instance, giving his age, height,
weight, chest and bicep measurements and asking which
member of the Shell or Fourth Form he most exactly resembles. The demand for a list of the studies on the Shell
passage, with an exact account of who lives in each, is a
very common one. The editors, of course, do everything
in their power to keep up the illusion. In the *Gem* Jack
Blake is supposed to write the answers to correspondents,
and in the *Magnet* a couple of pages is always given up to
the school magazine (the *Greyfriars Herald*, edited by
Harry Wharton), and there is another page in which one
or other character is written up each week. The stories run
in cycles, two or three characters being kept in the fore-
ground for several weeks at a time. First there will be a
series of rollicking adventure stories, featuring the Famous Five and Billy Bunter; then a run of stories turning
on mistaken identity, with Wibley (the make-up wizard)
in the star part; then a run of more serious stories in which

Vernon-Smith is trembling on the verge of expulsion. And here one comes upon the real secret of the *Gem* and *Magnet* and the probable reason why they continue to be read in spite of their obvious out-of-dateness.

It is that the characters are so carefully graded as to give almost every type of reader a character he can identify himself with. Most boys' papers aim at doing this, hence the boy-assistant (Sexton Blake's Tinker, Nelson Lee's Nipper, etc.) who usually accompanies the explorer, detective or what not on his adventures. But in these cases there is only one boy, and usually it is much the same type of boy. In the *Gem* and *Magnet* there is a model for very nearly everybody. There is the normal, athletic, high-spirited boy (Tom Merry, Jack Blake, Frank Nugent), a slightly rowdier version of this type (Bob Cherry), a more aristocratic version (Talbot, Manners), a quieter, more serious version (Harry Wharton), and a stolid, "bulldog" version (Johnny Bull). Then there is the reckless, dare-devil type of boy (Vernon-Smith), the definitely "clever," studious boy (Mark Linley, Dick Penfold), and the eccentric boy who is not good at games but possesses some special talent (Skinner, Wibley). And there is the scholarship-boy (Tom Redwing), an important figure in this class of story because he makes it possible for boys from very poor homes to project themselves into the public-school atmosphere. In addition there are Australian, Irish, Welsh, Manx, Yorkshire and Lancashire boys to play upon local patriotism. But the subtlety of characterisation goes deeper than this. If one studies the correspondence columns one sees that there is probably *no*

character in the *Gem* and *Magnet* whom some or other
reader does not identify with, except the out-and-out comics, Coker, Billy Bunter, Fisher T. Fish (the money-grubbing American boy) and, of course, the masters. Bunter,
though in his origin he probably owed something to the
fat boy in *Pickwick,* is a real creation. His tight trousers
against which boots and canes are constantly thudding,
his astuteness in search of food, his postal order which
never turns up, have made him famous wherever the Union
Jack waves. But he is not a subject for day-dreams. On
the other hand, another seeming figure of fun, Gussy (the
Honourable Arthur A. D'Arcy, "the swell of St. Jim's"),
is evidently much admired. Like everything else in the
*Gem* and *Magnet,* Gussy is at least thirty years out of
date. He is the "knut" of the early twentieth century or
even the "masher" of the 'nineties ("Bai Jove, deah boy!"
and "Weally, I shall be obliged to give you a feahful
thwashin'!"), the monocled idiot who made good on the
fields of Mons and Le Cateau. And his evident popularity
goes to show how deep the snob-appeal of this type is.
English people are extremely fond of the titled ass (cf.
Lord Peter Wimsey) who always turns up trumps in the
moment of emergency. Here is a letter from one of Gussy's
girl admirers:

> "I think you're too hard on Gussy. I wonder he's
> still in existence, the way you treat him. He's my
> hero. Did you know I write lyrics? How's this—to
> the tune of 'Goody Goody'?

"Gonna get my gas-mask, join the A.R.P.
'Cos I'm wise to all those bombs you drop on me.
Gonna dig myself a trench
Inside the garden fence;
Gonna seal my windows up with tin
So that the tear gas can't get in;
Gonna park my cannon right outside the kerb
With a note to Adolf Hitler: 'Don't disturb!'
And if I never fall in Nazi hands
That's soon enough for me
Gonna get my gas-mask, join the A.R.P.

"P.S.—Do you get on well with girls?"

I quote this in full because (dated April 1939) it is interesting as being probably the earliest mention of Hitler in the *Gem*. In the *Gem* there is also a heroic fat boy, Fatty Wynn, as a set-off against Bunter. Vernon-Smith, "the Bounder of the Remove," a Byronic character, always on the verge of the sack, is another great favourite. And even some of the cads probably have their following. Loder, for instance, "the rotter of the Sixth," is a cad, but he is also a highbrow and given to saying sarcastic things about football and the team spirit. The boys of the Remove only think him all the more of a cad for this, but a certain type of boy would probably identify with him. Even Racke, Crooke and Co. are probably admired by small boys who think it diabolically wicked to smoke cigarettes. (A frequent question in the correspondence column: "What brand of cigarettes does Racke smoke?")
Naturally the politics of the *Gem* and *Magnet* are Con-

servative, but in a completely pre-1914 style, with no
Fascist tinge. In reality their basic political assumptions
are two: nothing ever changes, and foreigners are funny.
In the *Gem* of 1939 Frenchmen are still Froggies and Italians are still Dagoes. Mossoo, the French master at
Greyfriars, is the usual comic-paper Frog, with pointed
beard, pegtop trousers, etc. Inky, the Indian boy, though
a rajah, and therefore possessing snob-appeal, is also the
comic babu of the *Punch* tradition. (" 'The rowfulness is
not the proper caper, my esteemed Bob,' said Inky. 'Let
dogs delight in the barkfulness and bitefulness, but the
soft answer is the cracked pitcher that goes longest to a
bird in the bush, as the English proverb remarks.' ")
Fisher T. Fish is the old-style stage Yankee (" 'Waal, I
guess,' " etc.) dating from a period of Anglo-American
jealousy. Wun Lung, the Chinese boy (he has rather
faded out of late, no doubt because some of the *Magnet's*
readers are Straits Chinese), is the nineteenth-century
pantomime Chinaman, with saucer-shaped hat, pigtail and
pidgin-English. The assumption all along is not only that
foreigners are comics who are put there for us to laugh at,
but that they can be classified in much the same way as
insects. That is why in all boys' papers, not only the *Gem*
and *Magnet*, a Chinese is invariably portrayed with a pigtail. It is the thing you recognise him by, like the Frenchman's beard or the Italian's barrel-organ. In papers of
this kind it occasionally happens that when the setting of
a story is in a foreign country some attempt is made to
describe the natives as individual human beings, but as a
rule it is assumed that foreigners of any one race are all

alike and will conform more or less exactly to the following patterns:

FRENCHMAN: Excitable. Wears beard, gesticulates wildly.

SPANIARD, MEXICAN, etc.: Sinister, treacherous.

ARAB, AFGHAN, etc.: Sinister, treacherous.

CHINESE: Sinister, treacherous. Wears pigtail.

ITALIAN: Excitable. Grinds barrel-organ or carries stiletto.

SWEDE, DANE, etc.: Kindhearted, stupid.

NEGRO: Comic, very faithful.

The working classes only enter into the *Gem* and *Magnet* as comics or semi-villains (race-course touts, etc.). As for class-friction, trade unionism, strikes, slumps, unemployment, Fascism and civil war—not a mention. Somewhere or other in the thirty years' issue of the two papers you might perhaps find the word "Socialism," but you would have to look a long time for it. If the Russian Revolution is anywhere referred to, it will be indirectly, in the word "Bolshy" (meaning a person of violent disagreeable habits). Hitler and the Nazis are just beginning to make their appearance, in the sort of reference I quoted above. The war-crisis of September 1938 made just enough impression to produce a story in which Mr. Vernon-Smith, the Bounder's millionaire father, cashed in on the general panic by buying up country houses in order to sell them to "crisis scuttlers." But that is probably as near to noticing the European situation as the *Gem* and *Magnet* will come,

until the war actually starts.[1] That does not mean that
these papers are unpatriotic—quite the contrary!
Throughout the Great War the *Gem* and *Magnet* were
perhaps the most consistently and cheerfully patriotic
papers in England. Almost every week the boys caught a
spy or pushed a conchy into the army, and during the
rationing period "EAT LESS BREAD" was printed in large
type on every page. But their patriotism has nothing
whatever to do with power-politics or "ideological" warfare. It is more akin to family loyalty, and actually it
gives one a valuable clue to the attitude of ordinary people, especially the huge untouched block of the middle
class and the better-off working class. These people are
patriotic to the middle of their bones, but they do not feel
that what happens in foreign countries is any of their
business. When England is in danger they rally to its defence as a matter of course, but in between-times they are
not interested. After all, England is always in the right
and England always wins, so why worry? It is an attitude
that has been shaken during the past twenty years, but
not so deeply as is sometimes supposed. Failure to understand it is one of the reasons why Left Wing political
parties are seldom able to produce an acceptable foreign
policy.

The mental world of the *Gem* and *Magnet*, therefore, is
something like this:

The year is 1910—or 1940, but it is all the same. You

[1] This was written some months before the outbreak of war.
Up to the end of September 1939 no mention of the war has appeared in either paper.

are at Greyfriars, a rosy-cheeked boy of fourteen in posh tailor-made clothes, sitting down to tea in your study on the Remove passage after an exciting game of football which was won by an odd goal in the last half-minute. There is a cosy fire in the study, and outside the wind is whistling. The ivy clusters thickly round the old grey stones. The King is on his throne and the pound is worth a pound. Over in Europe the comic foreigners are jabbering and gesticulating, but the grim grey battleships of the British Fleet are steaming up the Channel and at the outposts of Empire the monocled Englishmen are holding the natives at bay. Lord Mauleverer has just got another fiver and we are all settling down to a tremendous tea of sausages, sardines, crumpets, potted meat, jam and doughnuts. After tea we shall sit round the study fire having a good laugh at Billy Bunter and discussing the team for next week's match against Rookwood. Everything is safe, solid and unquestionable. Everything will be the same for ever and ever. That approximately is the atmosphere.

But now turn from the *Gem* and *Magnet* to the more up-to-date papers which have appeared since the Great War. The truly significant thing is that they have more points of resemblance to the *Gem* and *Magnet* than points of difference. But it is better to consider the differences first.

There are eight of these newer papers, the *Modern Boy, Triumph, Champion, Wizard, Rover, Skipper, Hotspur* and *Adventure*. All of these have appeared since the Great War, but except for the *Modern Boy* none of them is less than five years old. Two papers which ought also to be mentioned briefly here, though they are not strictly in the same class as the rest, are the *Detective Weekly* and the *Thriller*, both owned by the Amalgamated Press. The *Detective Weekly* has taken over Sexton Blake. Both of these papers admit a certain amount of sex-interest into their stories, and though certainly read by boys, they are not aimed at them exclusively. All the others are boys' papers pure and simple, and they are sufficiently alike to be considered together. There does not seem to be any notable difference between Thomson's publications and those of the Amalgamated Press.

As soon as one looks at these papers one sees their technical superiority to the *Gem* and *Magnet*. To begin with, they have the great advantage of not being written entirely by one person. Instead of one long complete story, a number of the *Wizard* or *Hotspur* consists of half a dozen or more serials, none of which goes on for ever. Consequently there is far more variety and far less padding, and none of the tiresome stylisation and facetiousness of the *Gem* and *Magnet*. Look at these two extracts, for example:

"Billy Bunter groaned.

"A quarter of an hour had elapsed out of the two hours that Bunter was booked for extra French.

"In a quarter of an hour there were only fifteen minutes! But every one of those minutes seemed inordinately long to Bunter. They seemed to crawl by like tired snails.

"Looking at the clock in Class-room No. 10 the fat

Owl could hardly believe that only fifteen minutes
had passed. It seemed more like fifteen hours, if not
fifteen days!

"Other fellows were in extra French as well as
Bunter. They did not matter. Bunter did!" (the
*Magnet*).

"After a terrible climb, hacking out handholds in
the smooth ice every step of the way up, Sergeant
Lionheart Logan of the Mounties was now clinging
like a human fly to the face of an icy cliff, as smooth
and treacherous as a giant pane of glass.

"An Arctic blizzard, in all its fury, was buffeting
his body, driving the blinding snow into his face,
seeking to tear his fingers loose from their handholds
and dash him to death on the jagged boulders which
lay at the foot of the cliff a hundred feet below.

"Crouching among those boulders were eleven villainous trappers who had done their best to shoot
down Lionheart and his companion, Constable Jim
Rogers—until the blizzard had blotted the two
Mounties out of sight from below." (the *Wizard*).

The second extract gets you some distance with the
story, the first takes a hundred words to tell you that Bunter is in the detention class. Moreover, by not concentrat-
ing on school stories (in point of numbers the school story
slightly predominates in all these papers, except the
*Thriller* and *Detective Weekly*), the *Wizard, Hotspur*,
etc., have far greater opportunities for sensationalism.
Merely looking at the cover illustrations of the papers

which I have on the table in front of me, here are some of the things I see. On one a cowboy is clinging by his toes to the wing of an aeroplane in mid-air and shooting down another aeroplane with his revolver. On another a Chinese is swimming for his life down a sewer with a swarm of ravenous-looking rats swimming after him. On another an engineer is lighting a stick of dynamite while a steel robot feels for him with its claws. On another a man in airman's costume is fighting barehanded against a rat somewhat larger than a donkey. On another a nearly naked man of terrific muscular development has just seized a lion by the tail and flung it thirty yards over the wall of an arena, with the words, "Take back your blooming lion!" Clearly no school story can compete with this kind of thing. From time to time the school buildings may catch fire or the French master may turn out to be the head of an international anarchist gang, but in a general way the interest must centre round cricket, school rivalries, practical jokes, etc. There is not much room for bombs, death-rays, sub-machine guns, aeroplanes, mustangs, octopuses, grizzly bears or gangsters.

Examination of a large number of these papers shows that, putting aside school stories, the favourite subjects are Wild West, Frozen North, Foreign Legion, crime (always from the detective's angle), the Great War (Air Force or Secret Service, not the infantry), the Tarzan motif in varying forms, professional football, tropical exploration, historical romance (Robin Hood, Cavaliers and Roundheads, etc.) and scientific invention. The Wild West still leads, at any rate as a setting, though the Red Indian

seems to be fading out. The one theme that is really new is
the scientific one. Death-rays, Martians, invisible men,
robots, helicopters and interplanetary rockets figure
largely; here and there there are èven far-off rumours of
psychotherapy and ductless glands. Whereas the *Gem* and
*Magnet* derive from Dickens and Kipling, the *Wizard,
Champion, Modern Boy,* etc., owe a great deal to H. G.
Wells, who, rather than Jules Verne, is the father of "Sci-
entifiction." Naturally it is the magical, Martian aspect
of science that is most exploited, but one or two papers
include serious articles on scientific subjects, besides quan-
tities of informative snippets. (Examples: "A Kauri tree
in Queensland, Australia, is over 12,000 years old";
"Nearly 50,000 thunderstorms occur every day"; "He-
lium gas costs £1 per 1000 cubic feet"; "There are over
500 varieties of spiders in Great Britain"; "London fire-
men use 14,000,000 gallons of water annually," etc. etc.)
There is a marked advance in intellectual curiosity and, on
the whole, in the demand made on the reader's attention.
In practice the *Gem* and *Magnet* and the post-war papers
are read by much the same public, but the mental age
aimed at seems to have risen by a year or two years—an
improvement probably corresponding to the improvement
in elementary education since 1909.

The other thing that has emerged in the post-war boys'
papers, though not to anything like the extent one would
expect, is bully-worship and the cult of violence.

If one compares the *Gem* and *Magnet* with a genuinely
modern paper, the thing that immediately strikes one is
the absence of the leader-principle. There is no central

dominating character; instead there are fifteen or twenty characters, all more or less on an equality, with whom readers of different types can identify. In the more modern papers this is not usually the case. Instead of identifying with a schoolboy of more or less his own age, the reader of the *Skipper, Hotspur,* etc., is led to identify with a G-man, with a Foreign Legionary, with some variant of Tarzan, with an air ace, a master spy, an explorer, a pugilist—at any rate with some single all-powerful character who dominates everyone about him and whose usual method of solving any problem is a sock on the jaw. This character is intended as a superman, and as physical strength is the form of power that boys can best understand, he is usually a sort of human gorilla; in the Tarzan type of story he is sometimes actually a giant, eight or ten feet high. At the same time the scenes of violence in nearly all these stories are remarkably harmless and unconvincing. There is a great difference in tone between even the most bloodthirsty English paper and the threepenny Yank Mags, *Fight Stories, Action Stories,* etc. (not strictly boys' papers, but largely read by boys). In the Yank Mags you get real blood-lust, really gory descriptions of the all-in, jump-on-his-testicles style of fighting, written in a jargon that has been perfected by people who brood endlessly on violence. A paper like *Fight Stories,* for instance, would have very little appeal except to sadists and masochists. You can see the comparative gentleness of the English civilisation by the amateurish way in which prize-fighting is always described in the boys' weeklies. There is no specialised vocabulary. Look at these four extracts, two English, two American:

"When the gong sounded, both men were breathing heavily, and each had great red marks on his chest. Bill's chin was bleeding, and Ben had a cut over his right eye.

"Into their corners they sank, but when the gong clanged again they were up swiftly, and they went like tigers at each other" (*Rover*).

"He walked in stolidly and smashed a clublike right to my face. Blood spattered and I went back on my heels, but surged in and ripped my right under the heart. Another right smashed full on Sven's already battered mouth, and, spitting out the fragments of a tooth, he crashed a flailing left to my body" (*Fight Stories*).

"It was amazing to watch the Black Panther at work. His muscles rippled and slid under his dark skin. There was all the power and grace of a giant cat in his swift and terrible onslaught.

"He volleyed blows with a bewildering speed for so huge a fellow. In a moment Ben was simply blocking with his gloves as well as he could. Ben was really a past-master of defence. He had many fine victories behind him. But the Negro's rights and lefts crashed through openings that hardly any other fighter could have found" (*Wizard*).

"Haymakers which packed the bludgeoning weight of forest monarchs crashing down under the ax hurled into the bodies of the two heavies as they swapped punches" (*Fight Stories*).

Notice how much more knowledgeable the American extracts sound. They are written for devotees of the prizering, the others are not. Also, it ought to be emphasised that on its level the moral code of the English boys' papers is a decent one. Crime and dishonesty are never held up to admiration, there is none of the cynicism and corruption of the American gangster story. The huge sale of the Yank Mags in England shows that there is a demand for that kind of thing, but very few English writers seem able to produce it. When hatred of Hitler became a major emotion in America, it was interesting to see how promptly "anti-Fascism" was adapted to pornographic purposes by the editors of the Yank Mags. One magazine which I have in front of me is given up to a long, complete story, "When Hell Came to America," in which the agents of a "blood-maddened European dictator" are trying to conquer the U.S.A. with death-rays and invisible aeroplanes. There is the frankest appeal to sadism, scenes in which the Nazis tie bombs to women's backs and fling them off heights to watch them blown to pieces in mid-air, others in which they tie naked girls together by their hair and prod them with knives to make them dance, etc. etc. The editor comments solemnly on all this, and uses it as a plea for tightening up restrictions against immigrants. On another page of the same paper: "LIVES OF THE HOT-CHA CHORUS GIRLS. Reveals all the intimate secrets and fascinating pastimes of the famous Broadway Hotcha

girls. NOTHING IS OMITTED. Price 10c." "HOW TO LOVE.
10c." "FRENCH PHOTO RING, 25c." "NAUGHTY NUDIES
TRANSFERS. From the outside of the glass you see a beautiful girl, innocently dressed. Turn it around and look
through the glass and oh! what a difference! Set of
3 transfers 25c.," etc. etc. etc. There is nothing at all like
this in any English paper likely to be read by boys. But
the process of Americanisation is going on all the same.
The American ideal, the "he-man," the "tough guy," the
gorilla who puts everything right by socking everybody
else on the jaw, now figures in probably a majority of
boys' papers. In one serial now running in the *Skipper* he
is always portrayed, ominously enough, swinging a rubber
truncheon.

The development of the *Wizard*, *Hotspur*, etc., as
against the earlier boys' papers, boils down to this: better
technique, more scientific interest, more bloodshed, more
leader-worship. But, after all, it is the *lack* of development that is the really striking thing.

To begin with, there is no political development whatever. The world of the *Skipper* and the *Champion* is still
the pre-1914 world of the *Magnet* and the *Gem*. The Wild
West story, for instance, with its cattle-rustlers, lynch-
law and other paraphernalia belonging to the 'eighties, is
a curiously archaic thing. It is worth noticing that in
papers of this type it is always taken for granted that adventures only happen at the ends of the earth, in tropical
forests, in Arctic wastes, in African deserts, on Western
prairies, in Chinese opium dens—everywhere, in fact, except the places where things really *do* happen. That is a

belief dating from thirty or forty years ago, when the new
continents were in process of being opened up. Nowadays,
of course, if you really want adventure, the place to look
for it is in Europe. But apart from the picturesque side of
the Great War, contemporary history is carefully ex-
cluded. And except that Americans are now admired instead of being laughed at, foreigners are exactly the same
figures of fun that they always were. If a Chinese character appears, he is still the sinister pig-tailed opium-smug-
gler of Sax Rohmer; no indication that things have been
happening in China since 1912—no indication that a war
is going on there, for instance. If a Spaniard appears, he
is still a "dago" or "greaser" who rolls cigarettes and
stabs people in the back; no indication that things have
been happening in Spain. Hitler and the Nazis have not
yet appeared, or are barely making their appearance.
There will be plenty about them in a little while, but it will
be from a strictly patriotic angle (Britain *versus* Germany), with the real meaning of the struggle kept out of
sight as much as possible. As for the Russian Revolution,
it is extremely difficult to find any reference to it in any of
these papers. When Russia is mentioned at all it is usually
in an information snippet (example: "There are 29,000
centenarians in the U.S.S.R."), and any reference to the
Revolution is indirect and twenty years out of date. In one
story in the *Rover*, for instance, somebody has a tame bear,
and as it is a Russian bear, it is nicknamed Trotsky—obviously an echo of the 1917-23 period and not of recent con-
troversies. The clock has stopped at 1910. Britannia rules
the waves, and no one has heard of slumps, booms, unem-

ployment, dictatorships, purges or concentration camps.

And in social outlook there is hardly any advance. The snobbishness is somewhat less open than in the *Gem* and *Magnet*—that is the most one can possibly say. To begin with, the school story, always partly dependent on snob-appeal, is by no means eliminated. Every number of a boys' paper includes at least one school story, these stories slightly outnumbering the Wild Westerns. The very elaborate fantasy-life of the *Gem* and *Magnet* is not imitated and there is more emphasis on extraneous adventure, but the social atmosphere (old grey stones) is much the same. When a new school is introduced at the beginning of a story we are often told in just those words that "it was a very posh school." From time to time a story appears which is ostensibly directed *against* snobbery. The schol-arship-boy (cf. Tom Redwing in the *Magnet*) makes fairly frequent appearances, and what is essentially the same theme is sometimes presented in this form; there is great rivalry between two schools, one of which considers itself more "posh" than the other, and there are fights, practical jokes, football matches, etc., always ending in the discomfiture of the snobs. If one glances very super-ficially at some of these stories it is possible to imagine that a democratic spirit has crept into the boys' weeklies, but when one looks more closely one sees that they merely reflect the bitter jealousies that exist within the white-col-lar class. Their real function is to allow the boy who goes to a cheap private school (*not* a Council school) to feel that his school is just as "posh" in the sight of God as Winchester or Eton. The sentiment of school loyalty

("We're better than the fellows down the road"), a thing
almost unknown to the real working class, is still kept up.
As these stories are written by many different hands, they
do, of course, vary a good deal in tone. Some are reasonably free from snobbishness, in others money and pedi-
gree are exploited even more shamelessly than in the *Gem*
and *Magnet*. In one that I came across an actual *majority*
of the boys mentioned were titled.

Where working-class characters appear, it is usually
either as comics (jokes about tramps, convicts, etc.), or as
prize-fighters, acrobats, cowboys, professional footballers
and Foreign Legionaries—in other words, as adventurers.
There is no facing of the facts about working-class life, or,
indeed, about *working* life of any description. Very occasionally one may come across a realistic description of,
say, work in a coal-mine, but in all probability it will only
be there as the background of some lurid adventure. In
any case the central character is not likely to be a coal-
miner. Nearly all the time the boy who reads these papers
—in nine cases out of ten a boy who is going to spend his
life working in a shop, in a factory or in some subordinate
job in an office—is led to identify with people in positions
of command, above all with people who are never troubled
by shortage of money. The Lord Peter Wimsey figure, the
seeming idiot who drawls and wears a monocle but is always to the fore in moments of danger, turns up over and
over again. (This character is a great favourite in Secret
Service stories.) And, as usual, the heroic characters all
have to talk B.B.C.; they may talk Scottish or Irish or
American, but no one in a star part is ever permitted to

drop an aitch. Here it is worth comparing the social atmosphere of the boys' weeklies with that of the women's
weeklies, the *Oracle*, the *Family Star*, *Peg's Paper*, etc.

The women's papers are aimed at an older public and
are read for the most part by girls who are working for a
living. Consequently they are on the surface much more
realistic. It is taken for granted, for example, that nearly
everyone has to live in a big town and work at a more or
less dull job. Sex, so far from being taboo, is *the* subject.
The short, complete stories, the special feature of these
papers, are generally of the "came the dawn" type: the
heroine narrowly escapes losing her "boy" to a designing
rival, or the "boy" loses his job and has to postpone marriage, but presently gets a better job. The changeling
fantasy (a girl brought up in a poor home is "really" the
child of rich parents) is another favourite. Where sensationalism comes in, usually in the serials, it arises out of
the more domestic type of crime, such as bigamy, forgery
or sometimes murder; no Martians, death-rays or international anarchist gangs. These papers are at any rate
aiming at credibility, and they have a link with real life in
their correspondence columns, where genuine problems are
being discussed. Ruby M. Ayres's column of advice in the
*Oracle*, for instance, is extremely sensible and well written.
And yet the world of the *Oracle* and *Peg's Paper* is a pure
fantasy-world. It is the same fantasy all the time; pretending to be richer than you are. The chief impression
that one carries away from almost every story in these
papers is of a frightful, overwhelming "refinement." Ostensibly the characters are working-class people, but their

habits, the interiors of their houses, their clothes, their
outlook and, above all, their speech are entirely middle
class. They are all living at several pounds a week above
their income. And needless to say, that is just the impression that is intended. The idea is to give the bored factory-
girl or worn-out mother of five a dream-life in which she
pictures herself—not actually as a duchess (that convention has gone out) but as, say, the wife of a bank-mana-
ger. Not only is a five-to-six-pound-a-week standard of
life set up as the ideal, but it is tacitly assumed that that is
how working-class people really *do* live. The major facts
are simply not faced. It is admitted, for instance, that
people sometimes lose their jobs; but then the dark clouds
roll away and they get better jobs instead. No mention of
unemployment as something permanent and inevitable, no
mention of the dole, no mention of trade unionism. No
suggestion anywhere that there can be anything wrong
with the system *as a system;* there are only individual mis-
fortunes, which are generally due to somebody's wickedness and can in any case be put right in the last chapter.
Always the dark clouds roll away, the kind employer raises
Alfred's wages, and there are jobs for everybody except
the drunks. It is still the world of the *Wizard* and the
*Gem,* except that there are orange-blossoms instead of
machine-guns.

The outlook inculcated by all these papers is that of a
rather exceptionally stupid member of the Navy League
in the year 1910. Yes, it may be said, but what does it
matter? And in any case, what else do you expect?

Of course no one in his senses would want to turn the

so-called penny dreadful into a realistic novel or a Socialist tract. An adventure story must of its nature be more
or less remote from real life. But, as I have tried to make
clear, the unreality of the *Wizard* and the *Gem* is not so
artless as it looks. These papers exist because of a specialised demand, because boys at certain ages find it necessary
to read about Martians, death-rays, grizzly bears and
gangsters. They get what they are looking for, but they
get it wrapped up in the illusions which their future employers think suitable for them. To what extent people
draw their ideas from fiction is disputable. Personally I
believe that most people are influenced far more than they
would care to admit by novels, serial stories, films and so
forth, and that from this point of view the worst books are
often the most important, because they are usually the
ones that are read earliest in life. It is probable that many
people who would consider themselves extremely sophisticated and "advanced" are actually carrying through life
an imaginative background which they acquired in childhood from (for instance) Sapper and Ian Hay. If that is
so, the boys' twopenny weeklies are of the deepest importance. Here is the stuff that is read somewhere between
the ages of twelve and eighteen by a very large proportion,
perhaps an actual majority, of English boys, including
many who will never read anything else except newspapers; and along with it they are absorbing a set of beliefs which would be regarded as hopelessly out of date in
the Central Office of the Conservative Party. All the better because it is done indirectly, there is being pumped
into them the conviction that the major problems of our

time do not exist, that there is nothing wrong with *laissez-faire* capitalism, that foreigners are unimportant comics and that the British Empire is a sort of charity-concern which will last for ever. Considering who owns these papers, it is difficult to believe that this is unintentional. Of the twelve papers I have been discussing (*i.e.* twelve including the *Thriller* and *Detective Weekly*) seven are the property of the Amalgamated Press, which is one of the biggest press-combines in the world and controls more than a hundred different papers. The *Gem* and *Magnet*, therefore, are closely linked up with the *Daily Telegraph* and the *Financial Times*. This in itself would be enough to rouse certain suspicions, even if it were not obvious that the stories in the boys' weeklies are politically vetted. So it appears that if you feel the need of a fantasy-life in which you travel to Mars and fight lions barehanded (and what boy doesn't?), you can only have it by delivering yourself over, mentally, to people like Lord Camrose. For there is no competition. Throughout the whole of this run of papers the differences are negligible, and on this level no others exist. This raises the question, why is there no such thing as a left-wing boys' paper?

At first glance such an idea merely makes one slightly sick. It is so horribly easy to imagine what a left-wing boys' paper would be like, if it existed. I remember in 1920 or 1921 some optimistic person handing round Communist tracts among a crowd of public-school boys. The tract I received was of the question-and-answer kind:

*Q.* "Can a Boy Communist be a Boy Scout, Comrade?"
*A.* "No, Comrade."

*Q.* "Why, Comrade?"

*A.* "Because, Comrade, a Boy Scout must salute the Union Jack, which is the symbol of tyranny and oppression." Etc. etc.

Now, suppose that at this moment somebody started a left-wing paper deliberately aimed at boys of twelve or fourteen. I do not suggest that the whole of its contents would be exactly like the tract I have quoted above, but does anyone doubt that they would be *something* like it? Inevitably such a paper would either consist of dreary uplift or it would be under Communist influence and given over to adulation of Soviet Russia; in either case no normal boy would ever look at it. Highbrow literature apart, the whole of the existing left-wing Press, in so far as it is at all vigorously "left," is one long tract. The one Socialist paper in England which could live a week on its merits *as a paper* is the *Daily Herald*: and how much Socialism is there in the *Daily Herald?* At this moment, therefore, a paper with a "left" slant and at the same time likely to have an appeal to ordinary boys in their teens is something almost beyond hoping for.

But it does not follow that it is impossible. There is no clear reason why every adventure story should necessarily be mixed up with snobbishness and gutter patriotism. For, after all, the stories in the *Hotspur* and the *Modern Boy* are not Conservative tracts; they are merely adventure stories with a Conservative bias. It is fairly easy to imagine the process being reversed. It is possible, for instance, to imagine a paper as thrilling and lively as the

*Hotspur*, but with subject-matter and "ideology" a little more up to date. It is even possible (though this raises other difficulties) to imagine a women's paper at the same literary level as the *Oracle*, dealing in approximately the same kind of story, but taking rather more account of the realities of working-class life. Such things have been done before, though not in England. In the last years of the Spanish monarchy there was a large output in Spain of left-wing novelettes, some of them evidently of anarchist origin. Unfortunately at the time when they were appearing I did not see their social significance, and I lost the collection of them that I had, but no doubt copies would still be procurable. In get-up and style of story they were very similar to the English fourpenny novelette, except that their inspiration was "left." If, for instance, a story described police pursuing anarchists through the mountains, it would be from the point of view of the anarchists and not of the police. An example nearer to hand is the Soviet film *Chapaiev*, which has been shown a number of times in London. Technically, by the standards of the time when it was made, *Chapaiev* is a first-rate film, but mentally, in spite of the unfamiliar Russian background, it is not so very remote from Hollywood. The one thing that lifts it out of the ordinary is the remarkable performance by the actor who takes the part of the White officer (the fat one) —a performance which looks very like an inspired piece of gagging. Otherwise the atmosphere is familiar. All the usual paraphernalia is there—heroic fight against odds, escape at the last moment, shots of galloping horses, love interest, comic relief. The film is in fact a fairly ordinary

one, except that its tendency is "left." In a Hollywood film
of the Russian Civil War the Whites would probably be
angels and the Reds demons. In the Russian version the
Reds are angels and the Whites demons. That also is a
lie, but, taking the long view, it is a less pernicious lie than
the other.

Here several difficult problems present themselves. Their
general nature is obvious enough, and I do not want to
discuss them. I am merely pointing to the fact that, in
England, popular imaginative literature is a field that
left-wing thought has never begun to enter. *All* fiction
from the novels in the mushroom libraries downwards is
censored in the interests of the ruling class. And boys' fiction above all, the blood-and-thunder stuff which nearly
every boy devours at some time or other, is sodden in the
worst illusions of 1910. The fact is only unimportant if
one believes that what is read in childhood leaves no impression behind. Lord Camrose and his colleagues evidently believe nothing of the kind, and, after all, Lord
Camrose ought to know.                                    1939.

# WELLS, HITLER
# AND THE WORLD STATE

"In March or April, say the wiseacres, there is to be a stupendous knockout blow at Britain. . . . What Hitler has to do it with, I cannot imagine. His ebbing and dispersed military resources are now probably not so very much greater than the Italians' before they were put to the test in Greece and Africa."

"The German air power has been largely spent. It is behind the times and its first-rate men are mostly dead or disheartened or worn out."

"In 1914 the Hohenzollern army was the best in the world. Behind that screaming little defective in Berlin there is nothing of the sort. . . . Yet our military 'experts' discuss the waiting phantom. In their imaginations it is perfect in its equipment and invincible in discipline. Sometimes it is to strike a decisive 'blow' through Spain and North Africa and on, or march through the Balkans, march from the

Danube to Ankara, to Persia, to India, or 'crush Russia,' or 'pour' over the Brenner into Italy. The weeks pass and the phantom does none of these things —for one excellent reason. It does not exist to that extent. Most of such inadequate guns and munitions as it possessed must have been taken away from it and fooled away in Hitler's silly feints to invade Britain. And its raw jerry-built discipline is wilting under the creeping realisation that the Blitzkrieg is spent, and the war is coming home to roost."

THESE quotations are not taken from the *Cavalry Quarterly* but from a series of newspaper articles by Mr. H. G. Wells, written at the beginning of this year [1] and now reprinted in a book entitled *Guide to the New World*. Since they were written, the German Army has overrun the Balkans and reconquered Cyrenaica, it can march through Turkey or Spain at such time as may suit it, and it has undertaken the invasion of Russia. How that campaign will turn out I do not know, but 'it is worth noticing that the German general staff, whose opinion is probably worth something, would not have begun it if they had not felt fairly certain of finishing it within three months. So much for the idea that the German Army is a bogey, its equipment inadequate, its morale breaking down, etc. etc.

What has Wells to set against the "screaming little defective in Berlin"? The usual rigmarole about a World State, plus the Sankey Declaration, which is an attempted definition of fundamental human rights, or anti-totali-

[1]    1945. *i.e.* at the beginning of 1941.

tarian tendency. Except that he is now especially concerned with federal world control of air power, it is the
same gospel as he has been preaching almost without inter-
ruption for the past forty years, always with an air of
angry surprise at the human beings who can fail to grasp
anything so obvious.

What is the use of saying that we need federal world
control of the air? The whole question is how we are to get
it. What is the use of pointing out that a World State is
desirable? What matters is that not one of the five great
military powers would think of submitting to such a thing.
All sensible men for decades past have been substantially
in agreement with what Mr. Wells says; but the sensible
men have no power and, in too many cases, no disposition
to sacrifice themselves. Hitler is a criminal lunatic, and
Hitler has an army of millions of men, aeroplanes in thousands, tanks in tens of thousands. For his sake a great nation has been willing to overwork itself for six years and
then to fight for two years more, whereas for the common-
sense, essentially hedonistic world-view which Mr. Wells
puts forward, hardly a human creature is willing to shed a
pint of blood. Before you can even talk of world recon-
struction, or even of peace, you have got to eliminate Hitler, which means bringing into being a dynamic not necessarily the same as that of the Nazis, but probably quite as
unacceptable to "enlightened" and hedonistic people.
What has kept England on its feet during the past year?
In part, no doubt, some vague idea about a better future,
but chiefly the atavistic emotion of patriotism, the in-
grained feeling of the English-speaking peoples that they

are superior to foreigners. For the last twenty years the
main object of English left-wing intellectuals has been to
break this feeling down, and if they had succeeded, we
might be watching the S.S. men patrolling the London
streets at this moment. Similarly, why are the Russians
fighting like tigers against the German invasion? In part,
perhaps, for some half-remembered ideal of Utopian Socialism, but chiefly in defence of Holy Russia (the "sacred
soil of the Fatherland," etc. etc.), which Stalin has revived
in an only slightly altered form. The energy that actually
shapes the world springs from emotions—racial pride,
leader-worship, religious belief, love of war—which liberal
intellectuals mechanically write off as anachronisms, and
which they have usually destroyed so completely in themselves as to have lost all power of action.

The people who say that Hitler is Antichrist, or alter-
natively, the Holy Ghost, are nearer an understanding of
the truth than the intellectuals who for ten dreadful years
have kept it up that he is merely a figure out of comic
opera, not worth taking seriously. All that this idea really
reflects is the sheltered conditions of English life. The
Left Book Club was at bottom a product of Scotland
Yard, just as the Peace Pledge Union is a product of the
Navy. One development of the last ten years has been the
appearance of the "political book," a sort of enlarged
pamphlet combining history with political criticism, as an
important literary form. But the best writers in this line
—Trotsky, Rauschning, Rosenberg, Silone, Borkenau,
Koestler and others—have none of them been Englishmen,
and nearly all of them have been renegades from one or

other extremist party, who have seen totalitarianism at close quarters and known the meaning of exile and persecution. Only in the English-speaking countries was it fashionable to believe, right up to the outbreak of war, that Hitler was an unimportant lunatic and the German tanks made of cardboard. Mr. Wells, it will be seen from the quotations I have given above, believes something of the kind still. I do not suppose that either the bombs or the German campaign in Greece have altered his opinion. A lifelong habit of thought stands between him and an understanding of Hitler's power.

Mr. Wells, like Dickens, belongs to the non-military middle class. The thunder of guns, the jingle of spurs, the catch in the throat when the old flag goes by, leave him manifestly cold. He has an invincible hatred of the fighting, hunting, swashbuckling side of life, symbolised in all his early books by a violent propaganda against horses. The principal villain of his *Outline of History* is the military adventurer, Napoleon. If one looks through nearly any book that he has written in the last forty years one finds the same idea constantly recurring: the supposed antithesis between the man of science who is working towards a planned World State and the reactionary who is trying to restore a disorderly past. In novels, Utopias, essays, films, pamphlets, the antithesis crops up, always more or less the same. On the one side science, order, progress, internationalism, aeroplanes, steel, concrete, hygiene: on the other side war, nationalism, religion, monarchy, peasants, Greek professors, poets, horses. History as he sees it is a series of victories won by the scientific man over the romantic man. Now, he is probably right in assuming that a "reasonable," planned form of society, with scientists rather than witch-doctors in control, will prevail sooner or later, but that is a different matter from assuming that it is just round the corner. There survives somewhere or other an interesting controversy which took place between Wells and Churchill at the time of the Russian Revolution. Wells accused Churchill of not really believing his own propaganda about the Bolsheviks being monsters dripping with blood, etc., but of merely fearing that they were going to introduce an era of common sense and scientific control, in which flag-wavers like Churchill himself would have no place. Churchill's estimate of the Bolsheviks, however, was nearer the mark than Wells's. The early Bolsheviks may have been angels or demons, according as one chooses to regard them, but at any rate they were not sensible men. They were not introducing a Wellsian Utopia but a Rule of the Saints, which, like the English Rule of the Saints, was a military despotism enlivened by witchcraft trials. The same misconception reappears in an inverted form in Wells's attitude to the Nazis. Hitler is all the war-lords and witch-doctors in history rolled into one. Therefore, argues Wells, he is an absurdity, a ghost from the past, a creature doomed to disappear almost immediately. But unfortunately the equation of science with common sense does not really hold good. The aeroplane, which was looked forward to as a civilising influence but in practice has hardly been used except for dropping bombs, is the symbol of that fact. Modern Germany is far more scientific than England, and far more barbarous.

Much of what Wells has imagined and worked for is physically there in Nazi Germany. The order, the planning, the State encouragement of science, the steel, the concrete, the aeroplanes, are all there, but all in the service of ideas appropriate to the Stone Age. Science is fighting on the side of superstition. But obviously it is impossible for Wells to accept this. It would contradict the world-view on which his own works are based. The war-lords and the witch-doctors *must* fail, the common-sense World State, as seen by a nineteenth-century Liberal whose heart does not leap at the sound of bugles, *must* triumph. Treachery and defeatism apart, Hitler *cannot* be a danger. That he should finally win would be an impossible reversal of history, like a Jacobite restoration.

But is it not a sort of parricide for a person of my age (thirty-eight) to find fault with H. G. Wells? Thinking people who were born about the beginning of this century are in some sense Wells's own creation. How much influence any mere writer has, and especially a "popular" writer whose work takes effect quickly, is questionable, but I doubt whether anyone who was writing books between 1900 and 1920, at any rate in the English language, influenced the young so much. The minds of all of us, and therefore the physical world, would be perceptibly different if Wells had never existed. Only, just the singleness of mind, the one-sided imagination that made him seem like an inspired prophet in the Edwardian age, make him a shallow, inadequate thinker now. When Wells was young, the antithesis between science and reaction was not false. Society was ruled by narrow-minded, profoundly incurious people, predatory business men, dull squires, bishops, politicians who could quote Horace but had never heard of algebra. Science was faintly disreputable and religious belief obligatory. Traditionalism, stupidity, snobbishness, patriotism, superstition and love of war seemed to be all on the same side; there was need of someone who could state the opposite point of view. Back in the nineteen-hundreds it was a wonderful experience for a boy to discover H. G. Wells. There you were, in a world of pedants, clergymen and golfers, with your future employers exhorting you to "get on or get out," your parents systematically warping your sexual life, and your dull-witted schoolmasters sniggering over their Latin tags; and here was this wonderful man who could tell you about the inhabitants of the planets and the bottom of the sea, and who *knew* that the future was not going to be what respectable people imagined. A decade or so before aeroplanes were technically feasible Wells knew that within a little while men would be able to fly. He knew that because he himself *wanted* to be able to fly, and therefore felt sure that research in that direction would continue. On the other hand, even when I was a little boy, at a time when the Wright brothers had actually lifted their machine off the ground for fifty-nine seconds, the generally accepted opinion was that if God had meant us to fly He would have given us wings. Up to 1914 Wells was in the main a true prophet. In physical details his vision of the new world has been fulfilled to a surprising extent.

But because he belonged to the nineteenth century and to a non-military nation and class, he could not grasp the

tremendous strength of the old world which was symbolised in his mind by fox-hunting Tories. He was, and
still is, quite incapable of understanding that nationalism,
religious bigotry and feudal loyalty are far more powerful
forces than what he himself would describe as sanity. Crea-
tures out of the Dark Ages have come marching into the
present, and if they are ghosts they are at any rate ghosts
which need a strong magic to lay them. The people who
have shown the best understanding of Fascism are either
those who have suffered under it or those who have a Fascist streak in themselves. A crude book like *The Iron Heel,*
written nearly thirty years ago, is a truer prophecy of the
future than either *Brave New World* or *The Shape of
Things to Come.* If one had to choose among Wells's own
contemporaries a writer who could stand towards him as
a corrective, one might choose Kipling, who was not deaf
to the evil voices of power and military "glory." Kipling
would have understood the appeal of Hitler, or for that
matter of Stalin, whatever his attitude towards them
might be. Wells is too sane to understand the modern
world. The succession of lower-middle-class novels which
are his greatest achievement stopped short at the other
war and never really began again, and since 1920 he has
squandered his talents in slaying paper dragons. But how
much it is, after all, to have any talents to squander.

**1941**

# THE ART
# OF DONALD McGILL

WHO does not know the "comics" of the cheap stationers'
windows, the penny or twopenny coloured post cards with
their endless succession of fat women in tight bathing-
dresses and their crude drawing and unbearable colours,
chiefly hedge-sparrow's egg tint and Post Office red?

This question ought to be rhetorical, but it is a curious
fact that many people seem to be unaware of the existence
of these things, or else to have a vague notion that they
are something to be found only at the seaside, like Negro
minstrels or peppermint rock. Actually they are on sale
everywhere—they can be bought at nearly any Wool-
worth's, for example—and they are evidently produced in
enormous numbers, new series constantly appearing. They
are not to be confused with the various other types of
comic illustrated post card, such as the sentimental ones
dealing with puppies and kittens or the Wendyish, sub-
pornographic ones which exploit the love-affairs of children. They are a *genre* of their own, specialising in very
"low" humour, the mother-in-law, baby's nappy, police-

men's boots type of joke, and distinguishable from all the other kinds by having no artistic pretensions. Some half-dozen publishing houses issue them, though the people who draw them seem not to be numerous at any one time.

I have associated them especially with the name of Donald McGill because he is not only the most prolific and by far the best of contemporary post card artists, but also the most representative, the most perfect in the tradition. Who Donald McGill is, I do not know. He is ˙apparently a trade name, for at least one series of post cards is issued simply as "The Donald McGill Comics," but he is also unquestionably a real person with a style of drawing which is recognisable at a glance. Anyone who examines his post cards in bulk will notice that many of them are not despicable even as drawings, but it would be mere dilettantism to pretend that they have any direct æsthetic value. A comic post card is simply an illustration to a joke, invariably a "low" joke, and it stands or falls by its ability to raise a laugh. Beyond that it has only "ideological" interest. McGill is a clever draughtsman with a real caricaturist's touch in the drawing of faces, but the special value of his post cards is that they are so completely typical. They represent, as it were, the norm of the comic post card. Without being in the least imitative, they are exactly what comic post cards have been any time these last forty years, and from them the meaning and purpose of the whole *genre* can be inferred.

Get hold of a dozen of these things, preferably McGill's —if you pick out from a pile the ones that seem to you funniest, you will probably find that most of them are

McGill's—and spread them out on a table. What do you see?

Your first impression is of overpowering vulgarity. This is quite apart from the ever-present obscenity, and apart also from the hideousness of the colours. They have an utter lowness of mental atmosphere which comes out not only in the nature of the jokes but, even more, in the grotesque, staring, blatant quality of the drawings. The designs, like those of a child, are full of heavy lines and empty spaces, and all the figures in them, every gesture and attitude, are deliberately ugly, the faces grinning and vacuous, the women monstrously parodied, with bottoms like Hottentots. Your second impression, however, is of indefinable familiarity. What do these things remind you of? What are they so like? In the first place, of course, they remind you of the barely different post cards which you probably gazed at in your childhood. But more than this, what you are really looking at is something as traditional as Greek tragedy, a sort of sub-world of smacked bottoms and scrawny mothers-in-law which is a part of Western European consciousness. Not that the jokes, taken one by one, are necessarily stale. Not being debarred from smuttiness, comic post cards repeat themselves less often than the joke columns in reputable magazines, but their basic subject-matter, the *kind* of joke they are aiming at, never varies. A few are genuinely witty, in a Max Millerish style. Examples:

> "I like seeing experienced girls home."
> "But I'm not experienced!"
> "You're not home yet!"

"I've been struggling for years to get a fur coat.
How did you get yours?"

"I left off struggling."

Judge: "You are prevaricating, sir. Did you or
did you not sleep with this woman?"

Co-respondent: "Not a wink, my lord!"

In general, however, they are not witty but humorous,
and it must be said for McGill's post cards, in particular,
that the drawing is often a good deal funnier than the
joke beneath it. Obviously the outstanding characteristic
of comic post cards is their obscenity, and I must discuss
that more fully later. But I give here a rough analysis of
their habitual subject-matter, with such explanatory remarks as seem to be needed:

*Sex.*—More than half, perhaps three-quarters, of the
jokes are sex jokes, ranging from the harmless to the all
but unprintable. First favourite is probably the illegitimate baby. Typical captions: "Could you exchange this
lucky charm for a baby's feeding-bottle?" "She didn't ask
me to the christening, so I'm not going to the wedding."
Also newlyweds, old maids, nude statues and women in
bathing-dresses. All of these are *ipso facto* funny, mere
mention of them being enough to raise a laugh. The cuck-
oldry joke is very seldom exploited, and there are no references to homosexuality.

Conventions of the sex joke:

(i) Marriage only benefits the women. Every
    man is plotting seduction and every

woman is plotting marriage. No woman
ever remains unmarried voluntarily.

(ii) Sex-appeal vanishes at about the age of
twenty-five. Well-preserved and good-
looking people beyond their first youth
are never represented. The amorous
honey-mooning couple reappear as the
grim-visaged wife and shapeless, mous-
tachioed, red-nosed husband, no intermediate stage being allowed for.

*Home life.*—Next to sex, the henpecked husband is the
favourite joke. Typical caption: "Did they get an X-ray
of your wife's jaw at the hospital?"—"No, they got a
moving picture instead."

Conventions:

(i) There is no such thing as a happy marriage.

(ii) No man ever gets the better of a woman in
argument.

*Drunkenness.*—Both drunkenness and teetotalism are
*ipso facto* funny.

Conventions:

(i) All drunken men have optical illusions.

(ii) Drunkenness is something peculiar to middle-aged men. Drunken youths or women
are never represented.

*W. C. jokes.*—There is not a large number of these.
Chamberpots are *ipso facto* funny, and so are public lava-

tories. A typical post card, captioned "A Friend in Need," shows a man's hat blown off his head and disappearing down the steps of a ladies' lavatory.

*Inter-working-class snobbery.*—Much in these post cards suggests that they are aimed at the better-off working class and poorer middle class. There are many jokes turning on malapropisms, illiteracy, dropped aitches and the rough manners of slum-dwellers. Countless post cards show draggled hags of the stage-charwoman type exchanging "unladylike" abuse. Typical repartee: "I wish you were a statue and I was a pigeon!" A certain number produced since the war treat evacuation from the anti-evacuee angle. There are the usual jokes about tramps, beggars and criminals, and the comic maidservant appears fairly frequently. Also the comic navvy, bargee, etc.; but there are no anti trade union jokes. Broadly speaking, everyone with much over or much under £5 a week is regarded as laughable. The "swell" is almost as automatically a figure of fun as the slum-dweller.

*Stock figures.*—Foreigners seldom or never appear. The chief locality joke is the Scotsman, who is almost inexhaustible. The lawyer is always a swindler, the clergyman always a nervous idiot who says the wrong thing. The "knut" or "masher" still appears, almost as in Edwardian days, in out-of-date-looking evening-clothes and an opera hat, or even with spats and a knobby cane. Another survival is the Suffragette, one of the big jokes of the pre-1914 period and too valuable to be relinquished. She has reappeared, unchanged in physical appearance, as the Feminist lecturer or Temperance fanatic. A feature of the last few years is the complete absence of anti-Jew post cards. The "Jew joke," always somewhat more ill-natured than the "Scotch joke," disappeared abruptly soon after the rise of Hitler.

*Politics.*—Any contemporary event, cult or activity which has comic possibilities (for example, "free love," feminism, A.R.P., nudism) rapidly finds its way into the picture post cards, but their general atmosphere is extremely old-fashioned. The implied political outlook is a Radicalism appropriate to about the year 1900. At normal times they are not only not patriotic, but go in for a mild guying of patriotism, with jokes about "God save the King," the Union Jack, etc. The European situation only began to reflect itself in them at some time in 1939, and first did so through the comic aspects of A.R.P. Even at this date few post cards mention the war except in A.R.P. jokes (fat woman stuck in the mouth of Anderson shelter: wardens neglecting their duty while young woman undresses at window she has forgotten to black out, etc. etc.). A few express anti-Hitler sentiments of a not very vindictive kind. One, not McGill's, shows Hitler, with the usual hypertrophied backside, bending down to pick a flower. Caption: "What would *you* do, chums?" This is about as high a flight of patriotism as any post card is likely to attain. Unlike the twopenny weekly papers, comic post cards are not the product of any great monopoly company, and evidently they are not regarded as having any importance in forming public opinion. There is no sign in them of any attempt to induce an outlook acceptable to the ruling class.

Here one comes back to the outstanding, all-important feature of comic post cards—their obscenity. It is by this that everyone remembers them, and it is also central to their purpose, though not in a way that is immediately obvious.

A recurrent, almost dominant motif in comic post cards is the woman with the stuck-out behind. In perhaps half of them, or more than half, even when the point of the joke has nothing to do with sex, the same female figure appears, a plump "voluptuous" figure with the dress clinging to it as tightly as another skin and with breasts or buttocks grossly over-emphasised, according to which way it is turned. There can be no doubt that these pictures lift the lid off a very widespread repression, natural enough in a country whose women when young tend to be slim to the point of skimpiness. But at the same time the McGill post card—and this applies to all other post cards in this *genre* —is not intended as pornography but, a subtler thing, as a skit on pornography. The Hottentot figures of the women are caricatures of the Englishman's secret ideal, not portraits of it. When one examines McGill's post cards more closely, one notices that his brand of humour only has meaning in relation to a fairly strict moral code. Whereas in papers like *Esquire,* for instance, or *La Vie Parisienne,* the imaginary background of the jokes is always promiscuity, the utter breakdown of all standards, the background of the McGill post card is marriage. The four leading jokes are nakedness, illegitimate babies, old maids and newly married couples, none of which would seem funny in a really dissolute or even "sophisticated" society. The post cards dealing with honeymoon couples always have the enthusiastic indecency of those village weddings where it is still considered screamingly funny to sew bells to the bridal bed. In one, for example, a young bridegroom is shown getting out of bed the morning after his wedding night. "The first morning in our own little home, darling!" he is saying; "I'll go and get the milk and paper and bring you up a cup of tea." Inset is a picture of the front doorstep; on it are four newspapers and four bottles of milk. This is obscene, if you like, but it is not immoral. Its implication—and this is just the implication the *Esquire* or the *New Yorker* would avoid at all costs— is that marriage is something profoundly exciting and important, the biggest event in the average human being's life. So also with jokes about nagging wives and tyrannous mothers-in-law. They do at least imply a stable society in which marriage is indissoluble and family loyalty taken for granted. And bound up with this is something I noted earlier, the fact that there are no pictures, or hardly any, of good-looking people beyond their first youth. There is the "spooning" couple and the middle-aged, cat-and-dog couple, but nothing in between. The liaison, the illicit but more or less decorous love-affair which used to be the stock joke of French comic papers, is not a post card subject. And this reflects, on a comic level, the working-class outlook which takes it as a matter of course that youth and adventure—almost, indeed, individual life— end with marriage. One of the few authentic class-differences, as opposed to class-distinctions, still existing in England is that the working classes age very much earlier.

They do not live less long, provided that they survive their childhood, nor do they lose their physical activity earlier, but they do lose very early their youthful appearance. This fact is observable everywhere, but can be most easily verified by watching one of the higher age groups registering for military service; the middle- and upper-class members look, on average, ten years younger than the others. It is usual to attribute this to the harder lives that the working classes have to live, but it is doubtful whether any such difference now exists as would account for it. More probably the truth is that the working classes reach middle age earlier because they accept it earlier. For to look young after, say, thirty is largely a matter of wanting to do so. This generalisation is less true of the better-paid workers, especially those who live in council houses and labour-saving flats, but it is true enough even of them to point to a difference of outlook. And in this, as usual, they are more traditional, more in accord with the Christian past than the well-to-do women who try to stay young at forty by means of physical jerks, cosmetics and avoidance of child-bearing. The impulse to cling to youth at all costs, to attempt to preserve your sexual attraction, to see even in middle age a future for yourself and not merely for your children, is a thing of recent growth and has only precariously established itself. It will probably disappear again when our standard of living drops and our birth-rate rises. "Youth's a stuff will not endure" expresses the normal, traditional attitude. It is this ancient wisdom that McGill and his colleagues are reflecting, no doubt unconsciously, when they allow for no transition stage between the honeymoon couple and those glamourless figures, Mum and Dad.

I have said that at least half McGill's post cards are sex jokes, and a proportion, perhaps ten per cent., are far more obscene than anything else that is now printed in England. Newsagents are occasionally prosecuted for selling them, and there would be many more prosecutions if the broadest jokes were not invariably protected by double meanings. A single example will be enough to show how this is done. In one post card, captioned "They didn't believe her," a young woman is demonstrating, with her hands held apart, something about two feet long to a couple of open-mouthed acquaintances. Behind her on the wall is a stuffed fish in a glass case, and beside that is a photograph of a nearly naked athlete. Obviously it is not the fish that she is referring to, but this could never be proved. Now, it is doubtful whether there is any paper in England that would print a joke of this kind, and certainly there is no paper that does so habitually. There is an immense amount of pornography of a mild sort, countless illustrated papers cashing in on women's legs, but there is no popular literature specialising in the "vulgar," farcical aspect of sex. On the other hand, jokes exactly like McGill's are the ordinary small change of the revue and music-hall stage, and are also to be heard on the radio, at moments when the censor happens to be nodding. In England the gap between what can be said and what can be printed is rather exceptionally wide. Remarks and gestures which hardly anyone objects to on the stage would raise a public outcry if any attempt were made to reproduce them on paper. (Compare Max Miller's stage patter with his weekly column in the *Sunday Dispatch.*) The comic post cards are the only existing exception to this rule, the only medium in which really "low" humour is considered to be printable. Only in post cards and on the variety stage can the stuck-out behind, dog and lamp-post, baby's nappy type of joke be freely exploited. Remembering that, one sees what function these post cards, in their humble way, are performing.

What they are doing is to give expression to the Sancho Panza view of life, the attitude to life that Miss Rebecca West once summed up as "extracting as much fun as possible from smacking behinds in basement kitchens." The Don Quixote-Sancho Panza combination, which of course is simply the ancient dualism of body and soul in fiction form, recurs more frequently in the literature of the last four hundred years than can be explained by mere imitation. It comes up again and again, in endless variations, Bouvard and Pécuchet, Jeeves and Wooster, Bloom and Dedalus, Holmes and Watson (the Holmes-Watson variant is an exceptionally subtle one, because the usual physical characteristics of two partners have been transposed). Evidently it corresponds to something enduring in our civilisation, not in the sense that either character is to be found in a "pure" state in real life, but in the sense that the two principles, noble folly and base wisdom, exist side by side in nearly every human being. If you look into your own mind, which are you, Don Quixote or Sancho Panza? Almost certainly you are both. There is one part of you that wishes to be a hero or a saint, but another part of you is a little fat man who sees very clearly the advantages of staying alive with a whole skin. He is your unofficial self, the voice of the belly protesting against the soul. His tastes lie towards safety, soft beds, no work, pots of beer and women with "voluptuous" figures. He it is who punctures your fine attitudes and urges you to look after Number One, to be unfaithful to your wife, to bilk your debts, and so on and so forth. Whether you allow yourself to be influenced by him is a different question. But it is simply a lie to say that he is not part of you, just as it is a lie to say that Don Quixote is not part of you either, though most of what is said and written consists of one lie or the other, usually the first.

But though in varying forms he is one of the stock figures of literature, in real life, especially in the way society is ordered, his point of view never gets a fair hearing. There is a constant world-wide conspiracy to pretend that he is not there, or at least that he doesn't matter. Codes of law and morals, or religious systems, never have much room in them for a humorous view of life. Whatever is funny is subversive, every joke is ultimately a custard pie, and the reason why so large a proportion of jokes centre round obscenity is simply that all societies, as the price of survival, have to insist on a fairly high standard of sexual morality. A dirty joke is not, of course, a serious attack upon morality, but it is a sort of mental rebellion, a momentary wish that things were otherwise. So also with all other jokes, which always centre round cowardice, laziness, dishonesty or some other quality which society cannot afford to encourage. Society has always to demand a little more from human beings than it will get in practice. It has to demand faultless discipline and self-sacrifice, it must expect its subjects to work hard, pay their taxes, and be faithful to their wives, it must assume that men think it glorious to die on the battlefield and women want to wear themselves out with child-bearing. The whole of what one may call official literature is founded on such assumptions. I never read the proclamations of generals before battle, the speeches of führers and prime ministers, the solidarity songs of public schools and Left Wing political parties, national anthems, Temperance tracts, papal encyclicals and sermons against gambling and contraception, without seeming to hear in the background a chorus of raspberries from all the millions of common men to whom these high sentiments make no appeal. Nevertheless the high sentiments always win in the end, leaders who offer blood, toil, tears and sweat always get more out of their followers than those who offer safety and a good time. When it comes to the pinch, human beings are heroic. Women face childbed and the scrubbing brush, revolutionaries keep their mouths shut in the torture chamber, battleships go down with their guns still firing when their decks are awash. It is only that the other element in man, the lazy, cowardly, debt-bilking adulterer who is inside all of us, can never be suppressed altogether and needs a hearing occasionally.

The comic post cards are one expression of his point of view, a humble one, less important than the music halls, but still worthy of attention. In a society which is still basically Christian they naturally concentrate on sex jokes; in a totalitarian society, if they had any freedom of expression at all, they would probably concentrate on laziness or cowardice, but at any rate on the unheroic in one form or another. It will not do to condemn them on the ground that they are vulgar and ugly. That is exactly what they are meant to be. Their whole meaning and virtue is in their unredeemed lowness, not only in the sense of obscenity, but lowness of outlook in every direction whatever. The slightest hint of "higher" influences would ruin them utterly. They stand for the worm's-eye view of life, for the music-hall world where marriage is a dirty joke or a comic disaster, where the rent is always behind and the clothes are always up the spout, where the lawyer is always a crook and the Scotsman always a miser, where the newly-weds make fools of themselves on the hideous beds of sea-side lodging-houses and the drunken, red-nosed husbands roll home at four in the morning to meet the linen-night-gowned wives who wait for them behind the front door, poker in hand. Their existence, the fact that people want them, is symptomatically important. Like the music halls, they are a sort of saturnalia, a harmless rebellion against virtue. They express only one tendency in the human mind, but a tendency which is always there and will find its own outlet, like water. On the whole, human beings want to be good, but not too good, and not quite all the time. For:

"there is a just man that perishes in his righteousness, and there is a wicked man that prolongeth his
life in his wickedness. Be not righteous over much;
neither make thyself over wise; why shouldst thou

destroy thyself? Be not overmuch wicked, neither be thou foolish: why shouldst thou die before thy time?"

In the past the mood of the comic post card could enter into the central stream of literature, and jokes barely different from McGill's could casually be uttered between the murders in Shakespeare's tragedies. That is no longer possible, and a whole category of humour, integral to our literature till 1800 or thereabouts, has dwindled down to these ill-drawn post cards, leading a barely legal existence in cheap stationers' windows. The corner of the human heart that they speak for might easily manifest itself in worse forms, and I for one should be sorry to see them vanish.                                                    1941.

# RUDYARD KIPLING

IT WAS a pity that Mr. Eliot should be so much on the defensive in the long essay with which he prefaces this selection of Kipling's poetry,[1] but it was not to be avoided, because before one can even speak about Kipling one has to clear away a legend that has been created by two sets of people who have not read his works. Kipling is in the peculiar position of having been a byword for fifty years. During five literary generations every enlightened person has despised him, and at the end of that time nine-tenths of those enlightened persons are forgotten and Kipling is in some sense still there. Mr. Eliot never satisfactorily explains this fact, because in answering the shallow and familiar charge that Kipling is a "Fascist," he falls into the opposite error of defending him where he is not defensible. It is no use pretending that Kipling's view of life, as a whole, can be accepted or even forgiven by any civilised person. It is no use claiming, for instance, that when Kipling describes a British soldier beating a "nig-

[1] *A Choice of Kipling's Verse,* made by T. S. Eliot (Faber & Faber, London).

ger" with a cleaning rod in order to get money out of him,
he is acting merely as a reporter and does not necessarily
approve what he describes. There is not the slightest sign
anywhere in Kipling's work that he disapproves of that
kind of conduct—on the contrary, there is a definite strain
of sadism in him, over and above the brutality which a
writer of that type has to have. Kipling *is* a jingo imperialist, he *is* morally insensitive and æsthetically disgusting. It is better to start by admitting that, and then to try
to find out why it is that he survives while the refined people who have sniggered at him seem to wear so badly.

And yet the "Fascist" charge has to be answered, because the first clue to any understanding of Kipling,
morally or politically, is the fact that he was *not* a Fascist.
He was further from being one than the most humane or
the most "progressive" person is able to be nowadays. An
interesting instance of the way in which quotations are
parroted to and fro without any attempt to look up their
context or discover their meaning is the line from "Re-
cessional," "Lesser breeds without the Law." This line is
always good for a snigger in pansy-left circles. It is assumed as a matter of course that the "lesser breeds" are
"natives," and a mental picture is called up of some pukka
sahib in a pith helmet kicking a coolie. In its context the
sense of the line is almost the exact opposite of this. The
phrase "lesser breeds" refers almost certainly to the Germans, and especially the pan-German writers, who are
"without the Law" in the sense of being lawless, not in the
sense of being powerless. The whole poem, conventionally
thought of as an orgy of boasting, is a denunciation of

power politics, British as well as German. Two stanzas are worth quoting (I am quoting this as politics, not as poetry):

"If, drunk with sight of power, we loose
Wild tongues that have not Thee in awe,
Such boastings as the Gentiles use,
Or lesser breeds without the Law—
Lord God of hosts, be with us yet,
Lest we forget—lest we forget!

"For heathen heart that puts her trust
In reeking tube and iron shard,
All valiant dust that builds on dust,
And guarding, calls not Thee to guard,
For frantic boast and foolish word—
Thy mercy on Thy People, Lord!"

Much of Kipling's phraseology is taken from the Bible, and no doubt in the second stanza he had in mind the text from Psalm cxxvii.: "Except the Lord build the house, they labour in vain that build it; except the Lord keep the city, the watchman waketh but in vain." It is not a text that makes much impression on the post-Hitler mind. No one, in our time, believes in any sanction greater than military power; no one believes that it is possible to overcome force except by greater force. There is no "law," there is only power. I am not saying that that is a true belief, merely that it is the belief which all modern men do actually hold. Those who pretend otherwise are either intellectual cowards, or power-worshippers under a thin disguise, or have simply not caught up with the age they are living in. Kipling's outlook is pre-Fascist. He still believes that pride comes before a fall and that the gods punish *hubris*. He does not foresee the tank, the bombing plane, the radio and the secret police, or their psychological results.

But in saying this, does not one unsay what I said above about Kipling's jingoism and brutality? No, one is merely saying that the nineteenth-century imperialist outlook and the modern gangster outlook are two different things. Kipling belongs very definitely to the period 1885–1902. The Great War and its aftermath embittered him, but he shows little sign of having learned anything from any event later than the Boer War. He was the prophet of British Imperialism in its expansionist phase (even more than his poems, his solitary novel, *The Light that Failed*, gives you the atmosphere of that time) and also the unofficial historian of the British Army, the old mercenary army which began to change its shape in 1914. All his confidence, his bouncing vulgar vitality, sprang out of limitations which no Fascist or near-Fascist shares.

Kipling spent the later part of his life in sulking, and no doubt it was political disappointment rather than literary vanity that accounted for this. Somehow history had not gone according to plan. After the greatest victory she had ever known, Britain was a lesser world power than before, and Kipling was quite acute enough to see this. The virtue had gone out of the classes he idealised, the young were hedonistic or disaffected, the desire to paint the map red had evaporated. He could not understand what was happening, because he had never had any grasp of the

economic forces underlying imperial expansion. It is notable that Kipling does not seem to realise, any more than
the average soldier or colonial administrator, that an empire is primarily a money-making concern. Imperialism as
he sees it is a sort of forcible evangelising. You turn a
Gatling gun on a mob of unarmed "natives," and then you
establish "the Law," which includes roads, railways and a
court-house. He could not foresee, therefore, that the same
motives which brought the Empire into existence would
end by destroying it. It was the same motive, for example,
that caused the Malayan jungles to be cleared for rubber
estates, and which now causes those estates to be handed
over intact to the Japanese. The modern totalitarians
know what they are doing, and the nineteenth-century
English did not know what they were doing. Both attitudes have their advantages, but Kipling was never able to
move forward from one into the other. His outlook, allowing for the fact that after all he was an artist, was that of
the salaried bureaucrat who despises the "box-wallah" and
often lives a lifetime without realising that the "box-wallah" calls the tune.

But because he identifies himself with the official class,
he does possess one thing which "enlightened" people seldom or never possess, and that is a sense of responsibility.
The middle-class Left hate him for this quite as much as
for his cruelty and vulgarity. All left-wing parties in the
highly industrialised countries are at bottom a sham, because they make it their business to fight against something which they do not really wish to destroy. They have
internationalist aims, and at the same time they struggle

to keep up a standard of life with which those aims are incompatible. We all live by robbing Asiatic coolies, and those of us who are "enlightened" all maintain that those coolies ought to be set free; but our standard of living, and hence our "enlightenment," demands that the robbery shall continue. A humanitarian is always a hypocrite, and Kipling's understanding of this is perhaps the central secret of his power to create telling phrases. It would be difficult to hit off the one-eyed pacifism of the English in fewer words than in the phrase, "making mock of uniforms that guard you while you sleep." It is true that Kipling does not understand the economic aspect of the relationship between the highbrow and the blimp. He does not see that the map is painted red chiefly in order that the coolie may be exploited. Instead of the coolie he sees the Indian Civil Servant; but even on that plane his grasp of function, of who protects whom, is very sound. He sees clearly that men can only be highly civilised while other men, inevitably less civilised, are there to guard and feed them.

How far does Kipling really identify himself with the administrators, soldiers and engineers whose praises he sings? Not so completely as is sometimes assumed. He had travelled very widely while he was still a young man, he had grown up with a brilliant mind in mainly philistine surroundings, and some streak in him that may have been partly neurotic led him to prefer the active man to the sensitive man. The nineteenth-century Anglo-Indians, to name the least sympathetic of his idols, were at any rate people who did things. It may be that all that they did was evil, but they changed the face of the earth (it is instructive to look at a map of Asia and compare the railway system of India with that of the surrounding countries), whereas they could have achieved nothing, could not have maintained themselves in power for a single week, if the normal Anglo-Indian outlook had been that of, say, E. M. Forster. Tawdry and shallow though it is, Kipling's is the only literary picture that we possess of nineteenth-century Anglo-India, and he could only make it because he was just coarse enough to be able to exist and keep his mouth shut in clubs and regimental messes. But he did not greatly resemble the people he admired. I know from several private sources that many of the Anglo-Indians who were Kipling's contemporaries did not like or approve of him. They said, no doubt truly, that he knew nothing about India, and on the other hand, he was from their point of view too much of a highbrow. While in India he tended to mix with "the wrong" people, and because of his dark complexion he was wrongly suspected of having a streak of Asiatic blood. Much in his development is traceable to his having been born in India and having left school early. With a slightly different background he might have been a good novelist or a superlative writer of music-hall songs. But how true is it that he was a vulgar flag-waver, a sort of publicity agent for Cecil Rhodes? It is true, but it is not true that he was a yes-man or a timeserver. After his early days, if then, he never courted public opinion. Mr. Eliot says that what is held against him is that he expressed unpopular views in a popular style. This narrows the issue by assuming that "unpopular" means unpopular with the intelligentsia, but it is a fact that Kipling's "message" was one that the big public did not want, and, indeed, has never accepted. The mass of the people, in the 'nineties as now, were anti-militarist, bored by the Empire, and only unconsciously patriotic. Kipling's official admirers are and were the "service" middle class, the people who read *Blackwood's*. In the stupid early years of this century, the blimps, having at last discovered someone who could be called a poet and who was on their side, set Kipling on a pedestal, and some of his more sententious poems, such as "If," were given almost Biblical status. But it is doubtful whether the blimps have ever read him with attention, any more than they have read the Bible. Much of what he says they could not possibly approve. Few people who have criticised England from the inside have said bitterer things about her than this gutter patriot. As a rule it is the British working class that he is attacking, but not always. That phrase about "the flannelled fools at the wicket and the muddied oafs at the goal" sticks like an arrow to this day, and it is aimed at the Eton and Harrow match as well as the Cup-Tie Final. Some of the verses he wrote about the Boer War have a curiously modern ring, so far as their subject-matter goes. "Stellenbosch," which must have been written about 1902, sums up what every intelligent infantry officer was saying in 1918, or is saying now, for that matter.

Kipling's romantic ideas about England and the Empire might not have mattered if he could have held them without having the class-prejudices which at that time went with them. If one examines his best and most representative work, his soldier poems, especially *Barrack-Room Ballads*, one notices that what more than anything else spoils them is an underlying air of patronage. Kipling idealises the army officer, especially the junior officer, and that to an idiotic extent, but the private soldier, though lovable and romantic, has to be a comic. He is always made to speak in a sort of stylised Cockney, not very broad but with all the aitches and final "g's" carefully omitted. Very often the result is as embarrassing as the humorous recitation at a church social. And this accounts for the curious fact that one can often improve Kipling's poems, make them less facetious and less blatant, by simply going through them and transplanting them from Cockney into standard speech. This is especially true of his refrains, which often have a truly lyrical quality. Two examples will do (one is about a funeral and the other about a wedding) :

"So it's knock out your pipes and follow me!
    And it's finish up your swipes and follow me!
        Oh, hark to the big drum calling,
            Follow me—follow me home!"

and again:

"Cheer for the Sergeant's wedding—
    Give them one cheer more!
Grey gun-horses in the lando,
    And a rogue is married to a whore!"

Here I have restored the aitches, etc. Kipling ought to have known better. He ought to have seen that the two

closing lines of the first of these stanzas are very beautiful
lines, and that ought to have overriden his impulse to
make fun of a working-man's accent. In the ancient ballads the lord and the peasant speak the same language.
This is impossible to Kipling, who is looking down a dis-
torting class-perspective, and by a piece of poetic justice
one of his best lines is spoiled—for "follow me 'ome" is
much uglier than "follow me home." But even where it
makes no difference musically the facetiousness of his
stage Cockney dialect is irritating. However, he is more
often quoted aloud than read on the printed page, and
most people instinctively make the necessary alterations
when they quote him.

Can one imagine any private soldier, in the 'nineties or
now, reading *Barrack-Room Ballads* and feeling that here
was a writer who spoke for him? It is very hard to do so.
Any soldier capable of reading a book of verse would notice at once that Kipling is almost unconscious of the class
war that goes on in an army as much as elsewhere. It is not
only that he thinks the soldier comic, but that he thinks
him patriotic, feudal, a ready admirer of his officers and
proud to be a soldier of the Queen. Of course that is partly
true, or battles could not be fought, but "What have I
done for thee, England, my England?" is essentially a
middle-class query. Almost any working man would follow
it up immediately with "What has England done for me?"
In so far as Kipling grasps this, he simply sets it down to
"the intense selfishness of the lower classes" (his own
phrase). When he is writing not of British but of "loyal"
Indians he carries the "Salaam, sahib" motif to sometimes

disgusting lengths. Yet it remains true that he has far
more interest in the common soldier, far more anxiety that
he shall get a fair deal, than most of the "liberals" of his
day or our own. He sees that the soldier is neglected,
meanly underpaid and hypocritically despised by the people whose incomes he safeguards. "I came to realise," he
says in his posthumous memoirs, "the bare horrors of the
private's life, and the unnecessary torments he endured."
He is accused of glorifying war, and perhaps he does so,
but not in the usual manner, by pretending that war is a
sort of football match. Like most people capable of writing
battle poetry, Kipling had never been in battle, but his
vision of war is realistic. He knows that bullets hurt, that
under fire everyone is terrified, that the ordinary soldier
never knows what the war is about or what is happening
except in his own corner of the battlefield, and that British
troops, like other troops, frequently run away:

"I 'eard the knives be'ind me, but I dursn't face my man,
  Nor I don't know where I went to, 'cause I didn't stop
      to see,
  Till I 'eard a beggar squealin' out for quarter as 'e ran,
  An' I thought I knew the voice an'—it was me!"

Modernize the style of this, and it might have come out of
one of the debunking war books of the nineteen-twenties.
Or again:

"An' now the hugly bullets come peckin' through the dust,
  An' no one wants to face 'em, but every beggar must;
  So, like a man in irons, which isn't glad to go,

> They moves 'em off by companies uncommon stiff an'
> slow."

Compare this with:

> "Forward the Light Brigade!
> Was there a man dismayed?
> No! though the soldier knew
> Someone had blundered."

If anything, Kipling overdoes the horrors, for the wars of his youth were hardly wars at all by our standards. Perhaps that is due to the neurotic strain in him, the hunger for cruelty. But at least he knows that men ordered to attack impossible objectives *are* dismayed, and also that fourpence a day is not a generous pension.

How complete or truthful a picture has Kipling left us of the long-service, mercenary army of the late nineteenth century? One must say of this, as of what Kipling wrote about nineteenth-century Anglo-India, that it is not only the best but almost the only literary picture we have. He has put on record an immense amount of stuff that one could otherwise only gather from verbal tradition or from unreadable regimental histories. Perhaps his picture of army life seems fuller and more accurate than it is because any middle-class English person is likely to know enough to fill up the gaps. At any rate, reading the essay on Kipling that Mr. Edmund Wilson has just published,[1] I was struck by the number of things that are boringly familiar to

---

[1] Published in a volume of essays, *The Wound and the Bow.* (Houghton Mifflin, 1941).

us and seem to be barely intelligible to an American. But from the body of Kipling's early work there does seem to emerge a vivid and not seriously misleading picture of the old pre-machine-gun army—the sweltering barracks in Gibraltar or Lucknow, the red coats, the pipeclayed belts and the pillbox hats, the beer, the fights, the floggings, hangings and crucifixions, the bugle-calls, the smell of oats and horse-piss, the bellowing sergeants with foot-long moustaches, the bloody skirmishes, invariably mismanaged, the crowded troopships, the cholera-stricken camps, the "native" concubines, the ultimate death in the workhouse. It is a crude, vulgar picture, in which a patriotic music-hall term seems to have got mixed up with one of Zola's gorier passages, but from it future generations will be able to gather some idea of what a long-term volunteer army was like. On about the same level they will be able to learn something of British India in the days when motor-cars and refrigerators were unheard of. It is an error to imagine that we might have had better books on these subjects if, for example, George Moore, or Gissing, or Thomas Hardy, had had Kipling's opportunities. That is the kind of accident that cannot happen. It was not possible that nineteenth-century England should produce a book like *War and Peace*, or like Tolstoy's minor stories of army life, such as *Sebastopol* or *The Cossacks*, not because the talent was necessarily lacking but because no one with sufficient sensitiveness to write such books would ever have made the appropriate contacts. Tolstoy lived in a great military empire in which it seemed natural for almost any young man of family to spend a few years in the army, whereas the British Empire was and still is demilitarised to a degree which continental observers find almost incredible. Civilised men do not readily move away from the centres of civilisation, and in most languages there is a great dearth of what one might call colonial literature. It took a very improbable combination of circumstances to produce Kipling's gaudy tableau, in which Private Ortheris and Mrs. Hauksbee pose against a background of palm trees to the sound of temple bells, and one necessary circumstance was that Kipling himself was only half civilised.

Kipling is the only English writer of our time who has added phrases to the language. The phrases and neologisms which we take over and use without remembering their origin do not always come from writers we admire. It is strange, for instance, to hear the Nazi broadcasters referring to the Russian soldiers as "robots," thus unconsciously borrowing a word from a Czech democrat whom they would have killed if they could have laid hands on him. Here are half a dozen phrases coined by Kipling which one sees quoted in leaderettes in the gutter press or overhears in saloon bars from people who have barely heard his name. It will be seen that they all have a certain characteristic in common:

"East is East, and West is West.
The white man's burden.
What do they know of England who only England know?
The female of the species is more deadly than the male.

Somewhere East of Suez.
Paying the Dane-geld."

There are various others, including some that have out-
lived their context by many years. The phrase "killing
Kruger with your mouth," for instance, was current till
very recently. It is also possible that it was Kipling who
first let loose the use of the word "Huns" for Germans; at
any rate he began using it as soon as the guns opened fire
in 1914. But what the phrases I have listed above have in
common is that they are all of them phrases which one
utters semi-derisively (as it might be "For I'm to be
Queen o' the May, mother, I'm to be Queen o' the May"),
but which one is bound to make use of sooner or later.
Nothing could exceed the contempt of the *New Statesman*,
for instance, for Kipling, but how many times during the
Munich period did the *New Statesman* find itself quoting
that phrase about paying the Dane-geld? [1] The fact is
that Kipling, apart from his snack-bar wisdom and his
gift for packing much cheap picturesqueness into a few
words ("Palm and Pine"—"East of Suez"—"The Road
to Mandalay"), is generally talking about things that are

[1] 1945. On the first page of his recent book, *Adam and Eve*, Mr.
Middleton Murry quoted the well-known lines:
"There are nine and fifty ways
Of constructing tribal lays,
And every single one of them is right."
He attributes these lines to Thackeray. This is probably what is
known as a "Freudian error." A civilised person would prefer not
to quote Kipling—*i.e.* would prefer not to feel that it was Kipling
who had expressed his thought for him.

of urgent interest. It does not matter, from this point of view, that thinking and decent people generally find themselves on the other side of the fence from him. "White man's burden" instantly conjures up a real problem, even if one feels that it ought to be altered to "black man's burden." One may disagree to the middle of one's bones with the political attitude implied in "The Islanders," but one cannot say that it is a frivolous attitude. Kipling deals in thoughts which are both vulgar and permanent. This raises the question of his special status as a poet, or verse-writer.

Mr. Eliot describes Kipling's metrical work as "verse" and not "poetry," but adds that it is "*great* verse," and further qualifies this by saying that a writer can only be described as a "great verse-writer" if there is some of his work "of which we cannot say whether it is verse or poetry." Apparently Kipling was a versifier who occasionally wrote poems, in which case it was a pity that Mr. Eliot did not specify these poems by name. The trouble is that whenever an æsthetic judgment on Kipling's work seems to be called for, Mr. Eliot is too much on the defensive to be able to speak plainly. What he does not say, and what I think one ought to start by saying in any discussion of Kipling, is that most of Kipling's verse is so horribly vulgar that it gives one the same sensation as one gets from watching a third-rate music-hall performer recite "The Pigtail of Wu Fang Fu" with the purple limelight on his face, *and yet* there is much of it that is capable of giving pleasure to people who know what poetry means. At his worst, and also his most vital, in poems like "Gunga

Din" or "Danny Deever," Kipling is almost a shameful pleasure, like the taste for cheap sweets that some people secretly carry into middle life. But even with his best passages one has the same sense of being seduced by something spurious, and yet unquestionably seduced. Unless one is merely a snob and a liar it is impossible to say that no one who cares for poetry could get any pleasure out of such lines as:

"For the wind is in the palm trees, and the temple bells
    they say,
  'Come you back, you British soldier, come you back to
    Mandalay!' "

and yet those lines are not poetry in the same sense as "Felix Randal" or "When icicles hang by the wall" are poetry. One can, perhaps, place Kipling more satisfactorily than by juggling with the words "verse" and "poetry," if one describes him simply as a good bad poet. He is as a poet what Harriet Beecher Stowe was as a novelist. And the mere existence of work of this kind, which is perceived by generation after generation to be vulgar and yet goes on being read, tells one something about the age we live in.

There is a great deal of good bad poetry in English, all of it, I should say, subsequent to 1790. Examples of good bad poems—I am deliberately choosing diverse ones—are "The Bridge of Sighs," "When all the World is Young, Lad," "The Charge of the Light Brigade," Bret Harte's "Dickens in Camp," "The Burial of Sir John Moore," "Jenny Kissed Me," "Keith of Ravelston," "Casabianca."

All of these reek of sentimentality, and yet—not these
particular poems, perhaps, but poems of this kind, are
capable of giving true pleasure to people who can see
clearly what is wrong with them. One could fill a fair-
sized anthology with good bad poems, if it were not for
the significant fact that good bad poetry is usually too
well known to be worth reprinting. It is no use pretending
that in an age like our own, "good" poetry can have any
genuine popularity. It is, and must be, the cult of a very
few people, the least tolerated of the arts. Perhaps that
statement needs a certain amount of qualification. True
poetry can sometimes be acceptable to the mass of the
people when it disguises itself as something else. One can
see an example of this in the folk-poetry that England
still possesses, certain nursery rhymes and mnemonic
rhymes, for instance, and the songs that soldiers make up,
including the words that go to some of the bugle-calls. But
in general ours is a civilisation in which the very word
"poetry" evokes a hostile snigger or, at best, the sort of
frozen disgust that most people feel when they hear the
word "God." If you are good at playing the concertina
you could probably go into the nearest public bar and get
yourself an appreciative audience within five minutes. But
what would be the attitude of that same audience if you
suggested reading them Shakespeare's sonnets, for instance? Good bad poetry, however, can get across to the
most unpromising audiences if the right atmosphere has
been worked up beforehand. Some months back Churchill
produced a great effect by quoting Clough's "Endeavour"
in one of his broadcast speeches. I listened to this speech

among people who could certainly not be accused of caring for poetry, and I am convinced that the lapse into verse impressed them and did not embarrass them. But not even Churchill could have got away with it if he had quoted anything much better than this.

In so far as a writer of verse can be popular, Kipling has been and probably still is popular. In his own lifetime some of his poems travelled far beyond the bounds of the reading public, beyond the world of school prize-days, Boy Scout singsongs, limp-leather editions, pokerwork and calendars, and out into the yet vaster world of the music halls. Nevertheless, Mr. Eliot thinks it worth while to edit him, thus confessing to a taste which others share but are not always honest enough to mention. The fact that such a thing as good bad poetry can exist is a sign of the emotional overlap between the intellectual and the ordinary man. The intellectual *is* different from the ordinary man, but only in certain sections of his personality, and even then not all the time. But what is the peculiarity of a good bad poem? A good bad poem is a graceful monument to the obvious. It records in memorable form—for verse is a mnemonic device, among other things—some emotion which very nearly every human being can share. The merit of a poem like "When All the World is Young, Lad" is that, however sentimental it may be, its sentiment is "true" sentiment in the sense that you are bound to find yourself thinking the thought it expresses sooner or later; and then, if you happen to know the poem, it will come back into your mind and seem better than it did before. Such poems are a kind of rhyming proverb, and it is a fact that definitely popular poetry is usually gnomic or sententious. One example from Kipling will do:

> "White hands cling to the bridle rein,
> Slipping the spur from the booted heel;
> Tenderest voices cry 'Turn again!'
> Red lips tarnish the scabbarded steel:
> Down to Gehenna or up to the Throne,
> He travels the fastest who travels alone."

There is a vulgar thought vigorously expressed. It may not be true, but at any rate it is a thought that everyone thinks. Sooner or later you will have occasion to feel that he travels the fastest who travels alone, and there the thought is, ready made and, as it were, waiting for you. So the chances are that, having once heard this line, you will remember it.

One reason for Kipling's power as a good bad poet I have already suggested—his sense of responsibility, which made it possible for him to have a world-view, even though it happened to be a false one. Although he had no direct connection with any political party, Kipling was a Conservative, a thing that does not exist nowadays. Those who now call themselves Conservatives are either Liberals, Fascists or the accomplices of Fascists. He identified himself with the ruling power and not with the opposition. In a gifted writer this seems to us strange and even disgusting, but it did have the advantage of giving Kipling a certain grip on reality. The ruling power is always faced with the question, "In such and such circumstances, what would you *do*?", whereas the opposition is not obliged to

take responsibility or make any real decisions. Where it
is a permanent and pensioned opposition, as in England,
the quality of its thought deteriorates accordingly. Moreover, anyone who starts out with a pessimistic, reactionary
view of life tends to be justified by events, for Utopia
never arrives and "the gods of the copybook headings," as
Kipling himself put it, always return. Kipling sold out to
the British governing class, not financially but emotionally. This warped his political judgment, for the British
ruling class were not what he imagined, and it led him into
abysses of folly and snobbery, but he gained a corresponding advantage from having at least tried to imagine what
action and responsibility are like. It is a great thing in his
favour that he is not witty, not "daring," has no wish to
*épater les bourgeois*. He dealt largely in platitudes, and
since we live in a world of platitudes, much of what he said
sticks. Even his worst follies seem less shallow and less irritating than the "enlightened" utterances of the same
period, such as Wilde's epigrams or the collection of
cracker-mottoes at the end of *Man and Superman*.

1942.

# W. B. YEATS

ONE thing that Marxist criticism has not succeeded in doing is to trace the connection between "tendency" and literary style. The subject-matter and imagery of a book can be explained in sociological terms, but its texture seemingly cannot. Yet some such connection there must be. One knows, for instance, that a Socialist would not write like Chesterton or a Tory imperialist like Bernard Shaw, though *how* one knows it is not easy to say. In the case of Yeats, there must be some kind of connection between his wayward, even tortured style of writing and his rather sinister vision of life. Mr. Menon [1] is chiefly concerned with the esoteric philosophy underlying Yeats's work, but the quotations which are scattered all through his interesting book serve to remind one how artificial Yeats's manner of writing was. As a rule, this artificiality is accepted as Irishism, or Yeats is even credited with simplicity because he uses short words, but in fact one seldom comes on six consecutive lines of his verse in which there is not an

[1] *The Development of William Butler Yeats*, by V. K. Narayana Menon (Oliver & Boyd, London, 1942).

archaism or an affected turn of speech. To take the nearest example:

> "Grant me an old man's Frenzy,
> My self must I remake
> Till I am Timon and Lear
> Or that William Blake
> Who beat upon the wall
> Till Truth obeyed his call."

The unnecessary "that" imports a feeling of affectation, and the same tendency is present in all but Yeats's best passages. One is seldom long away from a suspicion of "quaintness," something that links up not only with the 'nineties, the Ivory Tower and the "calf covers of pissed-on green," but also with Rackham's drawings, Liberty art-fabrics and the *Peter Pan* never-never land, of which, after all, *The Happy Townland* is merely a more appetising example. This does not matter, because, on the whole, Yeats gets away with it, and if his straining after effect is often irritating, it can also produce phrases ("the chill, footless years," "the mackerel-crowded seas") which suddenly overwhelm one like a girl's face seen across a room. He is an exception to the rule that poets do not use poetical language:

> "How many centuries spent
> The sedentary soul
> In toils of measurement
> Beyond eagle or mole,

> Beyond hearing or seeing,
> Or Archimedes' guess,
> To raise into being
> That loveliness?"

Here he does not flinch from a squashy vulgar word like "loveliness," and after all it does not seriously spoil this wonderful passage. But the same tendencies, together with a sort of raggedness which is no doubt intentional, weaken his epigrams and polemical poems. For instance (I am quoting from memory) the epigram against the critics who damned *The Playboy of the Western World*:

> "Once when midnight smote the air
> Eunuchs ran through Hell and met
> On every crowded street to stare
> Upon great Juan riding by;
> Even like these to rail and sweat,
> Staring upon his sinewy thigh."

The power which Yeats has within himself gives him the analogy ready made and produces the tremendous scorn of the last line, but even in this short poem there are six or seven unnecessary words. It would probably have been deadlier if it had been neater.

Mr. Menon's book is incidentally a short biography of Yeats, but he is above all interested in Yeats's philosophical "system," which in his opinion supplies the subject-matter of more of Yeats's poems than is generally recognised. This system is set forth fragmentarily in various places, and at full length in *A Vision*, a privately

printed book which I have never read but which Mr.
Menon quotes from extensively. Yeats gave conflicting accounts of its origin, and Mr. Menon hints pretty broadly
that the "documents" on which it was ostensibly founded
were imaginary. Yeats's philosophical system, says Mr.
Menon, "was at the back of his intellectual life almost
from the beginning. His poetry is full of it. Without it his
later poetry becomes almost completely unintelligible."
As soon as we begin to read about the so-called system we
are in the middle of a hocus-pocus of Great Wheels,
gyres, cycles of the moon, reincarnation, disembodied
spirits, astrology and what-not. Yeats hedges as to the lit-
eralness with which he believed in all this, but he certainly
dabbled in spiritualism and astrology, and in earlier life
had made experiments in alchemy. Although almost buried
under explanations, very difficult to understand, about the
phases of the moon, the central idea of his philosophical
system seems to be our old friend, the cyclical universe, in
which everything happens over and over again. One has
not, perhaps, the right to laugh at Yeats for his mystical
beliefs—for I believe it could be shown that *some* degree of
belief in magic is almost universal—but neither ought one
to write such things off as mere unimportant eccentricities. It is Mr. Menon's perception of this that gives his
book its deepest interest. "In the first flush of admiration
and enthusiasm," he says, "most people dismissed the fan-
tastical philosophy as the price we have to pay for a great
and curious intellect. One did not quite realise where he
was heading. And those who did, like Pound and perhaps
Eliot, approved the stand that he finally took. The first

reaction to this did not come, as one might have expected, from the politically minded young English poets. They were puzzled because a less rigid or artificial system than that of *A Vision* might not have produced the great poetry of Yeats's last days." It might not, and yet Yeats's philosophy has some very sinister implications, as Mr. Menon points out.

Translated into political terms, Yeats's tendency is Fascist. Throughout most of his life, and long before Fascism was ever heard of, he had had the outlook of those who reach Fascism by the aristocratic route. He is a great hater of democracy, of the modern world, science, machinery, the concept of progress—above all, of the idea of human equality. Much of the imagery of his work is feudal, and it is clear that he was not altogether free from ordinary snobbishness. Later these tendencies took clearer shape and led him to "the exultant acceptance of authoritarianism as the only solution. Even violence and tyranny are not necessarily evil because the people, knowing not evil and good, would become perfectly acquiescent to tyranny. . . . Everything must come from the top. Nothing can come from the masses." Not much interested in politics, and no doubt disgusted by his brief incursions into public life, Yeats nevertheless makes political pronouncements. He is too big a man to share the illusions of Liberalism, and as early as 1920 he foretells in a justly famous passage ("The Second Coming") the kind of world that we have actually moved into. But he appears to welcome the coming age, which is to be "hierarchical, masculine, harsh, surgical," and is influenced both by Ezra Pound and by various Italian Fascist writers. He describes the new civilisation which he hopes and believes will arrive: "an aristocratic civilisation in its most completed form, every detail of life hierarchical, every great man's door crowded at dawn by petitioners, great wealth everywhere in a few men's hands, all dependent upon a few, up to the Emperor himself, who is a God dependent on a greater God, and everywhere, in Court, in the family, an inequality made law." The innocence of this statement is as interesting as its snobbishness. To begin with, in a single phrase, "great wealth in a few men's hands," Yeats lays bare the central reality of Fascism, which the whole of its propaganda is designed to cover up. The merely political Fascist claims always to be fighting for justice: Yeats, the poet, sees at a glance that Fascism means injustice, and acclaims it for that very reason. But at the same time he fails to see that the new authoritarian civilisation, if it arrives, will not be aristocratic, or what he means by aristocratic. It will not be ruled by noblemen with Van Dyck faces, but by anonymous millionaires, shiny-bottomed bureaucrats and murdering gangsters. Others who have made the same mistake have afterwards changed their views, and one ought not to assume that Yeats, if he had lived longer, would necessarily have followed his friend Pound, even in sympathy. But the tendency of the passage I have quoted above is obvious, and its complete throwing overboard of whatever good the past two thousand years have achieved is a disquieting symptom.

How do Yeats's political ideas link up with his leaning towards occultism? It is not clear at first glance why hatred of democracy and a tendency to believe in crystal-gazing should go together. Mr. Menon only discusses this rather shortly, but it is possible to make two guesses. To begin with, the theory that civilisation moves in recurring cycles is one way out for people who hate the concept of human equality. If it is true that "all this," or something like it, "has happened before," then science and the modern world are debunked at one stroke and progress becomes for ever impossible. It does not much matter if the lower orders are getting above themselves, for, after all, we shall soon be returning to an age of tyranny. Yeats is by no means alone in this outlook. If the universe is moving round on a wheel, the future must be foreseeable, perhaps even in some detail. It is merely a question of discovering the laws of its motion, as the early astronomers discovered the solar year. Believe that, and it becomes difficult not to believe in astrology or some similar system. A year before the war, examining a copy of *Gringoire*, the French Fascist weekly, much read by army officers, I found in it no less than thirty-eight advertisements of clairvoyants. Secondly, the very concept of occultism carries with it the idea that knowledge must be a secret thing, limited to a small circle of initiates. But the same idea is integral to Fascism. Those who dread the prospect of universal suffrage, popular education, freedom of thought, emancipation of women, will start off with a predilection towards secret cults. There is another link between Fascism and magic in the profound hostility of both to the Christian ethical code.

No doubt Yeats wavered in his beliefs and held at differ-

ent times many different opinions, some enlightened, some
not. Mr. Menon repeats for him Eliot's claim that he had
the longest period of development of any poet who has
ever lived. But there is one thing that seems constant, at
least in all of his work that I can remember, and that is his
hatred of modern Western civilisation and desire to return
to the Bronze Age, or perhaps to the Middle Ages. Like
all such thinkers, he tends to write in praise of ignorance.
The Fool in his remarkable play, *The Hour-Glass*, is a
Chestertonian figure, "God's fool" the "natural born innocent," who is always wiser than the wise man. The philosopher in the play dies on the knowledge that all his lifetime
of thought has been wasted (I am quoting from memory
again):

> "The stream of the world has changed its course,
>     And with the stream my thoughts have run
>     Into some cloudy, thunderous spring
>     That is its mountain-source;
>     Ay, to a frenzy of the mind,
>     That all that we have done's undone
>     Our speculation but as the wind."

Beautiful words, but by implication profoundly obscurantist and reactionary; for if it is really true that a village
idiot, as such, is wiser than a philosopher, then it would
be better if the alphabet had never been invented. Of
course, all praise of the past is partly sentimental, because
we do not live in the past. The poor do not praise poverty.
Before you can despise the machine, the machine must set
you free from brute labour. But that is not to say that

Yeats's yearning for a more primitive and more hierarchical age was not sincere. How much of all this is traceable to mere snobbishness, product of Yeats's own position as an impoverished offshoot of the aristocracy, is a different question. And the connection between his obscurantist opinions and his tendency towards "quaintness" of language remains to be worked out; Mr. Menon hardly touches upon it.

This is a very short book, and I would greatly like to see Mr. Menon go ahead and write another book on Yeats, starting where this one leaves off. "If the greatest poet of our times is exultantly ringing in an era of Fascism, it seems a somewhat disturbing symptom," he says on the last page, and leaves it at that. It *is* a disturbing symptom, because it is not an isolated one. By and large the best writers of our time have been reactionary in tendency, and though Fascism does not offer any real return to the past, those who yearn for the past will accept Fascism sooner than its probable alternatives. But there are other lines of approach, as we have seen during the past two or three years. The relationship between Fascism and the literary intelligentsia badly needs investigating, and Yeats might well be the starting-point. He is best studied by someone like Mr. Menon, who can approach a poet primarily as a poet, but who also knows that a writer's political and religious beliefs are not excrescences to be laughed away, but something that will leave their mark even on the smallest detail of his work.                    1943.

# BENEFIT OF CLERGY:
## SOME NOTES ON SALVADOR DALI

AUTOBIOGRAPHY is only to be trusted when it reveals something disgraceful. A man who gives a good account of himself is probably lying, since any life when viewed from the inside is simply a series of defeats. However, even the most flagrantly dishonest book (Frank Harris's autobiographical writings are an example) can without intending it give a true picture of its author. Dali's recently published *Life*[1] comes under this heading. Some of the incidents in it are flatly incredible, others have been rearranged and romanticised, and not merely the humiliation but the persistent *ordinariness* of everyday life has been cut out. Dali is even by his own diagnosis narcissistic, and his autobiography is simply a strip-tease act conducted in pink limelight. But as a record of fantasy, of the perversion of instinct that has been made possible by the machine age, it has great value.

Here, then, are some of the episodes in Dali's life, from

[1] *The Secret Life of Salvador Dali* (The Dial Press, 1942).

his earliest years onward. Which of them are true and which are imaginary hardly matters: the point is that this is the kind of thing that Dali would have *liked* to do.

When he is six years old there is some excitement over the appearance of Halley's comet:

> "Suddenly one of my father's office clerks appeared in the drawing-room doorway and announced that the comet could be seen from the terrace. . . . While crossing the hall I caught sight of my little three-year-old sister crawling unobtrusively through a doorway. I stopped, hesitated a second, then gave her a terrible kick in the head as though it had been a ball, and continued running, carried away with a 'delirious joy' induced by this savage act. But my father, who was behind me, caught me and led me down into his office, where I remained as a punishment till dinner-time."

A year earlier than this Dali had "suddenly, as most of my ideas occur," flung another little boy off a suspension bridge. Several other incidents of the same kind are recorded, including (this was when he was twenty-nine years old) knocking down and trampling on a girl "until they had to tear her, bleeding, out of my reach."

When he is about five he gets hold of a wounded bat which he puts into a tin pail. Next morning he finds that the bat is almost dead and is covered with ants which are devouring it. He puts it in his mouth, ants and all, and bites it almost in half.

When he is adolescent a girl falls desperately in love

with him. He kisses and caresses her so as to excite her as much as possible, but refuses to go further. He resolves to keep this up for five years (he calls it his "five-year plan"), enjoying her humiliation and the sense of power it gives him. He frequently tells her that at the end of five years he will desert her, and when the time comes he does so.

Till well into adult life he keeps up the practice of masturbation, and likes to do this, apparently, in front of a looking-glass. For ordinary purposes he is impotent, it appears, till the age of thirty of so. When he first meets his future wife, Gala, he is greatly tempted to push her off a precipice. He is aware that there is something that she wants him to do to her, and after their first kiss the confession is made:

> "I threw back Gala's head, pulling it by the hair, and trembling with complete hysteria, I commanded:
>
> " 'Now tell me what you want me to do with you! But tell me slowly, looking me in the eye, with the crudest, the most ferociously erotic words that can make both of us feel the greatest shame'!
>
> ". . . Then Gala, transforming the last glimmer of her expression of pleasure into the hard light of her own tyranny, answered:
>
> " 'I want you to kill me!' "

He is somewhat disappointed by this demand, since it is merely what he wanted to do already. He contemplates throwing her off the bell-tower of the Cathedral of Toledo, but refrains from doing so.

During the Spanish Civil War he astutely avoids taking sides, and makes a trip to Italy. He feels himself more and more drawn towards the aristocracy, frequents smart *salons*, finds himself wealthy patrons, and is photographed with the plump Vicomte de Noailles, whom he describes as his "Maecenas." When the European War approaches he has one preoccupation only: how to find a place which has good cookery and from which he can make a quick bolt if danger comes too near. He fixes on Bordeaux, and duly flees to Spain during the Battle of France. He stays in Spain long enough to pick up a few anti-red atrocity stories, then makes for America. The story ends in a blaze of respectability. Dali, at thirty-seven, has become a devoted husband, is cured of his aberrations, or some of them, and is completely reconciled to the Catholic Church. He is also, one gathers, making a good deal of money.

However, he has by no means ceased to take pride in the pictures of his Surrealist period, with titles like "The Great Masturbator," "Sodomy of a Skull with a Grand Piano," etc. There are reproductions of these all the way through the book. Many of Dali's drawings are simply representational and have a characteristic to be noted later. But from his Surrealist paintings and photographs the two things that stand out are sexual perversity and necrophilia. Sexual objects and symbols—some of them well known, like our old friend the high-heeled slipper, others, like the crutch and the cup of warm milk, patented by Dali himself—recur over and over again, and there is a fairly well-marked excretory motif as well. In his painting, *Le Jeu Lugubre*, he says, "the drawers bespattered with excrement were painted with such minute and realistic complacency that the whole little Surrealist group was anguished by the question: Is he coprophagic or not?" Dali adds firmly that he is *not*, and that he regards this aberration as "repulsive," but it seems to be only at that point that his interest in excrement stops. Even when he recounts the experience of watching a woman urinate standing up, he has to add the detail that she misses her aim and dirties her shoes. It is not given to any one person to have all the vices, and Dali also boasts that he is not homosexual, but otherwise he seems to have as good an outfit of perversions as anyone could wish for.

However, his most notable characteristic is his necrophilia. He himself freely admits to this, and claims to have been cured of it. Dead faces, skulls, corpses of animals occur fairly frequently in his pictures, and the ants which devoured the dying bat make countless reappearances. One photograph shows an exhumed corpse, far gone in decomposition. Another shows the dead donkeys putrefying on top of grand pianos which formed part of the Surrealist film, *Le Chien Andalou*. Dali still looks back on these donkeys with great enthusiasm.

> "I 'made up' the putrefaction of the donkeys with great pots of sticky glue which I poured over them. Also I emptied their eye-sockets and made them larger by hacking them out with scissors. In the same way I furiously cut their mouths open to make the rows of their teeth show to better advantage, and I added several jaws to each mouth, so that it would

appear that although the donkeys were already rotting they were vomiting up a little more of their own
death, above those other rows of teeth formed by the
keys of the black pianos."

And finally there is the picture—apparently some kind
of faked photograph—of "Mannequin rotting in a taxicab." Over the already somewhat bloated face and breast
of the apparently dead girl, huge snails were crawling. In
the caption below the picture Dali notes that these are
Burgundy snails—that is, the edible kind.

Of course, in this long book of 400 quarto pages there
is more than I have indicated, but I do not think that I
have given an unfair account of his moral atmosphere and
mental scenery. It is a book that stinks. If it were possible
for a book to give a physical stink off its pages, this one
would—a thought that might please Dali, who before
wooing his future wife for the first time rubbed himself
all over with an ointment made of goat's dung boiled up
in fish glue. But against this has to be set the fact that
Dali is a draughtsman of very exceptional gifts. He is
also, to judge by the minuteness and the sureness of his
drawings, a very hard worker. He is an exhibitionist and
a careerist, but he is not a fraud. He has fifty times more
talent than most of the people who would denounce his
morals and jeer at his paintings. And these two sets of
facts, taken together, raise a question which for lack of
any basis of agreement seldom gets a real discussion.

The point is that you have here a direct, unmistakable
assault on sanity and decency; and even—since some of

Dali's pictures would tend to poison the imagination like a pornographic postcard—on life itself. What Dali has done and what he has imagined is debatable, but in his outlook, his character, the bedrock decency of a human being does not exist. He is as anti-social as a flea. Clearly, such people are undesirable, and a society in which they can flourish has something wrong with it.

Now, if you showed this book, with its illustrations, to Lord Elton, to Mr. Alfred Noyes, to *The Times* leaderwriters who exult over the "eclipse of the highbrow"—in fact, to any "sensible" art-hating English person—it is easy to imagine what kind of response you would get. They would flatly refuse to see any merit in Dali whatever. Such people are not only unable to admit that what is morally degraded can be æsthetically right, but their real demand of every artist is that he shall pat them on the back and tell them that thought is unnecessary. And they can be especially dangerous at a time like the present, when the Ministry of Information and the British Council put power into their hands. For their impulse is not only to crush every new talent as it appears, but to castrate the past as well. Witness the renewed highbrow-baiting that is now going on in this country and America, with its outcry not only against Joyce, Proust and Lawrence, but even against T. S. Eliot.

But if you talk to the kind of person who *can* see Dali's merits, the response that you get is not as a rule very much better. If you say that Dali, though a brilliant draughtsman, is a dirty little scoundrel, you are looked upon as a savage. If you say that you don't like rotting corpses, and that people who do like rotting corpses are mentally diseased, it is assumed that you lack the æsthetic sense. Since "Mannequin rotting in a taxicab" is a good composition (as it undoubtedly is), it cannot be a disgusting, degrading picture; whereas Noyes, Elton, etc., would tell you that because it is disgusting it cannot be a good composition. And between these two fallacies there is no middle position; or, rather, there is a middle position, but we seldom hear much about it. On the one side *Kulturbolschewismus*: on the other (though the phrase itself is out of fashion) "Art for Art's sake." Obscenity is a very difficult question to discuss honestly. People are too frightened either of seeming to be shocked or of seeming not to be shocked, to be able to define the relationship between art and morals.

It will be seen that what the defenders of Dali are claiming is a kind of *benefit of clergy*. The artist is to be exempt from the moral laws that are binding on ordinary people. Just pronounce the magic word "Art," and everything is O.K. Rotting corpses with snails crawling over them are O.K.; kicking little girls in the head is O.K.; even a film like *L'Age d'Or* is O.K.[1] It is also O.K. that Dali should batten on France for years and then scuttle off like a rat as soon as France is in danger. So long as you can paint well enough to pass the test, all shall be forgiven you.

[1] Dali mentions *L'Age d'Or* and adds that its first public showing was broken up by hooligans, but he does not say in detail what it was about. According to Henry Miller's account of it, it showed among other things some fairly detailed shots of a woman defecating.

One can see how false this is if one extends it to cover ordinary crime. In an age like our own, when the artist is an altogether exceptional person, he must be allowed a certain amount of irresponsibility, just as a pregnant woman is. Still, no one would say that a pregnant woman should be allowed to commit murder, nor would anyone make such a claim for the artist, however gifted. If Shakespeare returned to the earth to-morrow, and if it were found that his favourite recreation was raping little girls in railway carriages, we should not tell him to go ahead with it on the ground that he might write another *King Lear*. And, after all, the worst crimes are not always the punishable ones. By encouraging necrophilic reveries one probably does quite as much harm as by, say, picking pockets at the races. One ought to be able to hold in one's head simultaneously the two facts that Dali is a good draughtsman and a disgusting human being. The one does not invalidate or, in a sense, affect the other. The first thing that we demand of a wall is that it shall stand up. If it stands up, it is a good wall, and the question of what purpose it serves is separable from that. And yet even the best wall in the world deserves to be pulled down if it surrounds a concentration camp. In the same way it should be possible to say, "This is a good book or a good picture, and it ought to be burned by the public hangman." Unless one can say that, at least in imagination, one is shirking the implications of the fact that an artist is also a citizen and a human being.

Not, of course, that Dali's autobiography, or his pictures, ought to be suppressed. Short of the dirty post cards that used to be sold in Mediterranean seaport towns, it is doubtful policy to suppress anything, and Dali's fantasies probably cast useful light on the decay of capitalist civilisation. But what he clearly needs is diagnosis. The question is not so much *what* he is as *why* he is like that. It ought not to be in doubt that he is a diseased intelligence, probably not much altered by his alleged conversion, since genuine penitents, or people who have returned to sanity, do not flaunt their past vices in that complacent way. He is a symptom of the world's illness. The important thing is not to denounce him as a cad who ought to be horsewhipped, or to defend him as a genius who ought not to be questioned, but to find out *why* he exhibits that particular set of aberrations.

The answer is probably discoverable in his pictures, and those I myself am not competent to examine. But I can point to one clue which perhaps takes one part of the distance. This is the old-fashioned, over-ornate, Edwardian style of drawing to which Dali tends to revert when he is not being Surrealist. Some of Dali's drawings are reminiscent of Dürer, one (p. 113) seems to show the influence of Beardsley, another (p. 269) seems to borrow something from Blake. But the most persistent strain is the Edwardian one. When I opened the book for the first time and looked at its innumerable marginal illustrations, I was haunted by a resemblance which I could not immediately pin down. I fetched up at the ornamental candlestick at the beginning of Part I (p. 7). What did this remind me of? Finally I tracked it down. It reminded me of a large, vulgar, expensively got-up edition of Anatole France (in translation) which must have been published about 1914. That had ornamental chapter headings and tailpieces after this style. Dali's candlestick displays at one end a curly fish-like creature that looks curiously familiar (it seems to be based on the conventional dolphin), and at the other is the burning candle. This candle, which recurs in one picture after another, is a very old friend. You will find it, with the same picturesque gouts of wax arranged on its sides, in those phoney electric lights done up as candlesticks which are popular in sham-Tudor country hotels. This candle, and the design beneath it, convey at once an intense feeling of sentimentality. As though to counteract this, Dali has spattered a quill-ful of ink all over the page, but without avail. The same impression keeps popping up on page after page. The design at the bottom of page 62, for instance, would nearly go into *Peter Pan*. The figure on page 224, in spite of having her cranium elongated into an immense sausage-like shape, is the witch of the fairy-tale books. The horse on page 234 and the unicorn on page 218 might be illustrations to James Branch Cabell. The rather pansified drawings of youths on pages 97, 100 and elsewhere convey the same impression. Picturesqueness keeps breaking in. Take away the skulls, ants, lobsters, telephones and other parapher-nalia, and every now and again you are back in the world of Barrie, Rackham, Dunsany and *Where the Rainbow Ends*.

Curiously enough, some of the naughty-naughty touches in Dali's autobiography tie up with the same period. When I read the passage I quoted at the begin-

ning, about the kicking of the little sister's head, I was
aware of another phantom resemblance. What was it? Of
course! *Ruthless Rhymes for Heartless Homes,* by Harry
Graham. Such rhymes were very popular round about
1912, and one that ran:

> "Poor little Willy is crying so sore,
> A sad little boy is he,
> For he's broken his little sister's neck
> And he'll have no jam for tea,"

might almost have been founded on Dali's anecdote. Dali,
of course, is aware of his Edwardian leanings, and makes
capital out of them, more or less in a spirit of pastiche. He
professes an especial affection for the year 1900, and
claims that every ornamental object of 1900 is full of
mystery, poetry, eroticism, madness, perversity, etc. Pastiche, however, usually implies a real affection for the
thing parodied. It seems to be, if not the rule, at any rate
distinctly common for an intellectual bent to be accom-
panied by a non-rational, even childish urge in the same
direction. A sculptor, for instance, is interested in planes
and curves, but he is also a person who enjoys the physical
act of mucking about with clay or stone. An engineer is a
person who enjoys the feel of tools, the noise of dynamos
and the smell of oil. A psychiatrist usually has a leaning
towards some sexual aberration himself. Darwin became a
biologist partly because he was a country gentleman and
fond of animals. It may be, therefore, that Dali's seemingly perverse cult of Edwardian things (for example, his
"discovery" of the 1900 subway entrances) is merely the

symptom of a much deeper, less conscious affection. The innumerable, beautifully executed copies of textbook illustrations, solemnly labelled *le rossignol, une montre* and so on, which he scatters all over his margins, may be meant partly as a joke. The little boy in knickerbockers playing with a diabolo on page 103 is a perfect period piece. But perhaps these things are also there because Dali can't help drawing that kind of thing because it is to that period and that style of drawing that he really belongs.

If so, his aberrations are partly explicable. Perhaps they are a way of assuring himself that he is not commonplace. The two qualities that Dali unquestionably possesses are a gift for drawing and an atrocious egoism. "At seven," he says in the first paragraph of his book, "I wanted to be Napoleon. And my ambition has been growing steadily ever since." This is worded in a deliberately startling way, but no doubt it is substantially true. Such feelings are common enough. "I knew I was a genius," somebody once said to me, "long before I knew what I was going to be a genius *about*." And suppose that you have nothing in you except your egoism and a dexterity that goes no higher than the elbow; suppose that your real gift is for a detailed, academic, representational style of drawing, your real *métier* to be an illustrator of scientific textbooks. How then do you become Napoleon?

There is always one escape: *into wickedness*. Always do the thing that will shock and wound people. At five, throw a little boy off a bridge, strike an old doctor across the face with a whip and break his spectacles—or, at any rate, dream about doing such things. Twenty years later, gouge the eyes out of dead donkeys with a pair of scissors. Along those lines you can always feel yourself original. And after all, it pays! It is much less dangerous than crime. Making all allowance for the probable suppressions in Dali's autobiography, it is clear that he has not had to suffer for his eccentricities as he would have done in an earlier age. He grew up into the corrupt world of the nineteen-twenties, when sophistication was immensely widespread and every European capital swarmed with aristocrats and *rentiers* who had given up sport and politics and taken to patronising the arts. If you threw dead donkeys at people, they threw money back. A phobia for grasshoppers—which a few decades back would merely have provoked a snigger—was now an interesting "complex" which could be profitably exploited. And when that particular world collapsed before the German Army, America was waiting. You could even top it all up with religious conversion, moving at one hop and without a shadow of repentance from the fashionable *salons* of Paris to Abraham's bosom.

That, perhaps, is the essential outline of Dali's history. But why his aberrations should be the particular ones they were, and why it should be so easy to "sell" such horrors as rotting corpses to a sophisticated public—those are questions for the psychologist and the sociological critic. Marxist criticism has a short way with such phenomena as Surrealism. They are "bourgeois decadence" (much play is made with the phrases "corpse poisons" and "decaying *rentier* class"), and that is that. But though this probably states a fact, it does not establish a connection. One would still like to know *why* Dali's leaning was towards necrophilia (and not, say, homosexuality), and *why* the *rentiers* and the aristocrats should buy his pictures instead of hunting and making love like their grandfathers. Mere moral disapproval does not get one any further. But neither ought one to pretend, in the name of "detachment," that such pictures as "Mannequin rotting in a taxicab" are morally neutral. They are diseased and disgusting, and any investigation ought to start out from that fact.                                                            1944.

# ARTHUR KOESTLER

ONE striking fact about English literature during the present century is the extent to which it has been dominated by foreigners—for example, Conrad, Henry James, Shaw, Joyce, Yeats, Pound and Eliot. Still, if you chose to make this a matter of national prestige and examine our achievement in the various branches of literature, you would find that England made a fairly good showing until you came to what may be roughly described as political writing, or pamphleteering. I mean by this the special class of literature that has arisen out of the European political struggle since the rise of Fascism. Under this heading novels, autobiographies, books of "reportage," sociological treatises and plain pamphlets can all be lumped together, all of them having a common origin and to a great extent the same emotional atmosphere.

Some of the outstanding figures in this school of writers are Silone, Malraux, Salvemini, Borkenau, Victor Serge and Koestler himself. Some of these are imaginative writers, some not, but they are all alike in that they are trying to write contemporary history, but *unofficial* history, the kind that is ignored in the text-books and lied about in the newspapers. Also they are all alike in being continental Europeans. It may be an exaggeration, but it cannot be a very great one, to say that whenever a book dealing with totalitarianism appears in this country, and still seems worth reading six months after publication, it is a book translated from some foreign language. English writers, over the past dozen years, have poured forth an enormous spate of political literature, but they have produced almost nothing of æsthetic value, and very little of historical value either. The Left Book Club, for instance, has been running ever since 1936. How many of its chosen volumes can you even remember the names of? Nazi Germany, Soviet Russia, Spain, Abyssinia, Austria, Czechoslovakia— all that these and kindred subjects have produced, in England, are slick books of reportage, dishonest pamphlets in which propaganda is swallowed whole and then spewed up again, half digested, and a very few reliable guide-books and text-books. There has been nothing resembling, for instance, *Fontamara* or *Darkness at Noon*, because there is almost no English writer to whom it has happened to see totalitarianism from the inside. In Europe, during the past decade and more, things have been happening to middle-class people which in England do not even happen to the working class. Most of the European writers I mentioned above, and scores of others like them, have been obliged to break the law in order to engage in politics at all; some of them have thrown bombs and fought in street-battles, many have been in prison or the concentration camp, or fled across frontiers with false names and forged passports. One cannot imagine, say Professor Laski indulging in activities of that kind. England is lacking, therefore, in what one might call concentration-camp literature. The special world created by secret police forces, censorship of opinion, torture and frame-up trials is, of course, known about and to some extent disapproved of, but it has made very little emotional impact. One result of this is that there exists in England almost no literature of disillusionment about the Soviet Union. There is the attitude of ignorant disapproval, and there is the attitude of uncritical admiration, but very little in between. Opinion on the Moscow sabotage trials, for instance, was divided, but divided chiefly on the question of whether the accused were guilty. Few people were able to see that, whether justified or not, the trials were an unspeakable horror. And English disapproval of the Nazi outrages has also been an unreal thing, turned on and off like a tap according to political expediency. To understand such things one has to be able to imagine oneself as the victim, and for an Englishman to write *Darkness at Noon* would be as unlikely an accident as for a slave-trader to write *Uncle Tom's Cabin.*

Koestler's published work really centres about the Moscow trials. His main theme is the decadence of revolutions owing to the corrupting effects of power, but the special nature of the Stalin dictatorship has driven him back into a position not far removed from pessimistic Conservatism. I do not know how many books he has written in all. He is a Hungarian who usually writes in German, and five books have been published in England: *Spanish Testament, The*

*Gladiators, Darkness at Noon, The Scum of the Earth,*
and *Arrival and Departure.* The subject-matter of all of
them is similar and none of them ever escapes for more
than a few pages from the atmosphere of nightmare. Of
the five books, the action of three takes place entirely or
almost entirely in prison.

In the opening months of the Spanish Civil War Koestler was the *News Chronicle's* correspondent in Spain,
and early in 1937 he was taken prisoner when the Fascists
captured Malaga. He was nearly shot out of hand, then
spent some months imprisoned in a fortress, listening
every night to the roar of rifle fire as batch after batch of
Republicans was executed, and being most of the time in
acute danger of execution himself. This was not a chance
adventure which "might have happened to anybody," but
was in accordance with Koestler's life style. A politically
indifferent person would not have been in Spain at that
date, a more cautious observer would have got out of
Malaga before the Fascists arrived, and a British or
American newspaper man would have been treated with
more consideration. The book that Koestler wrote about
this, *Spanish Testament,* has remarkable passages, but
apart from the scrappiness that is usual in a book of reportage, it is definitely false in places. In the prison scenes
Koestler successfully establishes the nightmare atmosphere
which is, so to speak, his patent, but the rest of the book is
too much coloured by the Popular Front orthodoxy of the
time. One or two passages even look as though they had
been doctored for the purposes of the Left Book Club. At
that time Koestler still was, or recently had been, a mem-

ber of the Communist Party, and the complex politics of
the Civil War made it impossible for any Communist to
write quite honestly about the internal struggle on the
Government side. The sin of nearly all left-wingers from
1933 onwards is that they have wanted to be anti-Fascist
without being anti-totalitarian. In 1937 Koestler already
knew this, but did not feel free to say so. He came much
nearer to saying it—indeed, he did say it, though he put
on a mask to do so—in his next book, *The Gladiators*,
which was published about a year before the war and for
some reason attracted very little attention.

*The Gladiators* is in some ways an unsatisfactory book.
It is about Spartacus, the Thracian gladiator who raised a
slaves' rebellion in Italy round about 65 B.C., and any
book on such a subject is handicapped by challenging
comparison with *Salâmmbo*. In our own age it would not
be possible to write a book like *Salâmmbo* even if one had
the talent. The great thing about *Salâmmbo*, even more
important than its physical detail, is its utter merciless-
ness. Flaubert could think himself into the stony cruelty
of antiquity, because in the mid-nineteenth century one
still had peace of mind. One had time to travel in the past.
Nowadays the present and the future are too terrifying to
be escaped from, and if one bothers with history it is in
order to find modern meanings there. Koestler makes
Spartacus into an allegorical figure, a primitive version
of the proletarian dictator. Whereas Flaubert has been
able, by a prolonged effort of the imagination, to make his
mercenaries truly pre-Christian, Spartacus is a modern
man dressed up. But this might not matter if Koestler

were fully aware of what his allegory means. Revolutions always go wrong—that is the main theme. It is on the question of *why* they go wrong that he falters, and his uncertainty enters into the story and makes the central figures enigmatic and unreal.

For several years the rebellious slaves are uniformly successful. Their numbers swell to a hundred thousand, they overrun great areas of Southern Italy, they defeat one punitive expedition after another, they ally themselves with the pirates who at that time were the masters of the Mediterranean, and finally they set to work to build a city of their own, to be named the City of the Sun. In this city human beings are to be free and equal, and above all, they are to be happy: no slavery, no hunger, no injustice, no floggings, no executions. It is the dream of a just society which seems to haunt the human imagination ineradicably and in all ages, whether it is called the Kingdom of Heaven or the classless society, or whether it is thought of as a Golden Age which once existed in the past and from which we have degenerated. Needless to say, the slaves fail to achieve it. No sooner have they formed themselves into a community than their way of life turns out to be as unjust, laborious and fear-ridden as any other. Even the cross, symbol of slavery, has to be revived for the punishment of malefactors. The turning-point comes when Spartacus finds himself obliged to crucify twenty of his oldest and most faithful followers. After that the City of the Sun is doomed, the slaves split up and are defeated in detail, the last fifteen thousand of them being captured and crucified in one batch.

The serious weakness of this story is that the motives of Spartacus himself are never made clear. The Roman lawyer Fulvius, who joins the rebellion and acts as its chronicler, sets forth the familiar dilemma of ends and means. You can achieve nothing unless you are willing to use force and cunning, but in using them you pervert your original aims. Spartacus, however, is not represented as power-hungry, nor, on the other hand, as a visionary. He is driven onwards by some obscure force which he does not understand, and he is frequently in two minds as to whether it would not be better to throw up the whole adventure and flee to Alexandria while the going is good. The slaves' republic is in any case wrecked rather by hedonism than by the struggle for power. The slaves are discontented with their liberty because they still have to work, and the final break-up happens because the more turbulent and less civilised slaves, chiefly Gauls and Germans, continue to behave like bandits after the republic has been established. This may be a true account of events—naturally we know very little about the slave rebellions of antiquity—but by allowing the Sun City to be destroyed because Crixus the Gaul cannot be prevented from looting and raping, Koestler has faltered between allegory and history. If Spartacus is the prototype of the modern revolutionary—and obviously he is intended as that—he should have gone astray because of the impossibility of combining power with righteousness. As it is, he is an almost passive figure, acted upon rather than acting, and at times not convincing. The story partly fails because the central problem of revolution has been avoided or, at least, has not been solved.

It is again avoided in a subtler way in the next book, Koestler's masterpiece, *Darkness at Noon*. Here, however, the story is not spoiled, because it deals with individuals and its interest is psychological. It is an episode picked out from a background that does not have to be questioned. *Darkness at Noon* describes the imprisonment and death of an Old Bolshevik, Rubashov, who first denies and ultimately confesses to crimes which he is well aware he has not committed. The grown-upness, the lack of surprise or denunciation, the pity and irony with which the story is told, show the advantage, when one is handling a theme of this kind, of being a European. The book reaches the stature of tragedy, whereas an English or American writer could at most have made it into a polemical tract. Koestler has digested his material and can treat it on the æsthetic level. At the same time his handling of it has a political implication, not important in this case but likely to be damaging in later books.

Naturally the whole book centres round one question: Why did Rubashov confess? He is not guilty—that is, not guilty of anything except the essential crime of disliking the Stalin regime. The concrete acts of treason in which he is supposed to have engaged are all imaginary. He has not even been tortured, or not very severely. He is worn down by solitude, toothache, lack of tobacco, bright lights glaring in his eyes, and continuous questioning, but these in themselves would not be enough to overcome a hardened revolutionary. The Nazis have previously done worse to him without breaking his spirit. The confessions obtained in the Russian State trials are capable of three explanations:

(1) That the accused were guilty.
(2) That they were tortured, and perhaps blackmailed by threats to relatives and friends.
(3) That they were actuated by despair, mental bankruptcy and the habit of loyalty to the Party.

For Koestler's purpose in *Darkness at Noon* (1) is ruled out, and though this is not the place to discuss the Russian purges, I must add that what little verifiable evidence there is suggests that the trials of the Old Bolsheviks were frame-ups. If one assumes that the accused were not guilty—at any rate, not guilty of the particular things they confessed to—then (2) is the common-sense explanation. Koestler, however, plumps for (3), which is also accepted by the Trotskyist Boris Souvarine, in his pamphlet *Cauchemar en URSS*. Rubashov ultimately confesses because he cannot find in his own mind any reason for not doing so. Justice and objective truth have long ceased to have any meaning for him. For decades he has been simply the creature of the Party, and what the Party now demands is that he shall confess to non-existent crimes. In the end, though he has had to be bullied and weakened first, he is somewhat proud of his decision to confess. He feels superior to the poor Czarist officer who inhabits the next cell and who talks to Rubashov by tapping on the wall. The Czarist officer is shocked when he learns that Rubashov intends to capitulate. As he sees it from his "bourgeois" angle, everyone ought to stick to his guns, even a Bolshevik. Honour, he says, consists in doing what you think right. "Honour is to be useful without fuss," Rubashov taps back; and he reflects with a certain satisfaction that he is tapping with his pince-nez while the other, the relic of the past, is tapping with a monocle.

Like Bukharin, Rubashov is "looking out upon black darkness." What is there, what code, what loyalty, what notion of good and evil, for the sake of which he can defy the Party and endure further torment? He is not only alone, he is also hollow. He has himself committed worse crimes than the one that is now being perpetrated against him. For example, as a secret envoy of the Party in Nazi Germany, he has got rid of disobedient followers by betraying them to the Gestapo. Curiously enough, if he has any inner strength to draw upon, it is the memories of his boyhood when he was the son of a landowner. The last thing he remembers, when he is shot from behind, is the leaves of the poplar trees on his father's estate. Rubashov belongs to the older generation of Bolsheviks that was largely wiped out in the purges. He is aware of art and literature, and of the world outside Russia. He contrasts sharply with Gletkin, the young G.P.U. man who conducts his interrogation, and who is the typical "good Party man," completely without scruples or curiosity, a thinking gramophone. Rubashov, unlike Gletkin, does not have the Revolution as his starting-point. His mind was not a blank sheet when the party got hold of it. His superiority to the other is finally traceable to his bourgeois origin.

One cannot, I think, argue that *Darkness at Noon* is simply a story dealing with the adventures of an imaginary individual. Clearly it is a political book, founded on history and offering an interpretation of disputed events. Rubashov might be Trotsky, Bukharin, Rakovsky or some other relatively civilised figure among the Old Bolsheviks. If one writes about the Moscow trials one must answer the question, "Why did the accused confess?" and which answer one makes is a political decision. Koestler answers, in effect, "Because these people had been rotted by the Revolution which they served," and in doing so he comes near to claiming that revolutions are of their nature bad. If one assumes that the accused in the Moscow trials were made to confess by means of some kind of terrorism, one is only saying that one particular set of revolutionary leaders has gone astray. Individuals, and not the situation, are to blame. The implication of Koestler's book, however, is that Rubashov in power would be no better than Gletkin: or rather, only better in that his outlook is still partly pre-revolutionary. Revolution, Koestler seems to say, is a corrupting process. Really enter into the Revolution and you must end up as either Rubashov or Gletkin. It is not merely that "power corrupts": so also do the ways of attaining power. Therefore, all efforts to regenerate society *by violent means* lead to the cellars of the Ogpu. Lenin leads to Stalin, and would have come to resemble Stalin if he had happened to survive.

Of course, Koestler does not say this quite explicitly, and perhaps is not altogether conscious of it. He is writing about darkness, but it is darkness at what ought to be

noon. Part of the time he feels that things might have
turned out differently. The notion that So-and-so has "be-
trayed," that things have only gone wrong because of individual wickedness, is ever present in left-wing thought.
Later, in *Arrival and Departure*, Koestler swings over
much further towards the anti-revolutionary position, but
in between these two books there is another, *The Scum of
the Earth*, which is straight autobiography and has only
an indirect bearing upon the problems raised by *Darkness
at Noon*. True to his life style, Koestler was caught in
France by the outbreak of war and, as a foreigner and a
known anti-Fascist, was promptly arrested and interned
by the Daladier Government. He spent the first nine
months of war mostly in a prison camp, then, during the
collapse of France, escaped and travelled by devious
routes to England, where he was once again thrown into
prison as an enemy alien. This time he was soon released,
however. The book is a valuable piece of reportage, and
together with a few other scraps of honest writing that
happened to be produced at the time of the debacle, it is a
reminder of the depths that bourgeois democracy can de-
scend to. At this moment, with France newly liberated and
the witch-hunt after collaborators in full swing, we are apt
to forget that in 1940 various observers on the spot considered that about forty per cent. of the French population
was either actively pro-German or completely apathetic.
Truthful war books are never acceptable to non-combat-
ants, and Koestler's book did not have a very good recep-
tion. Nobody came well out of it—neither the bourgeois
politicians, whose idea of conducting an anti-Fascist war

was to jail every left-winger they could lay hands on, nor the French Communists, who were effectively pro-Nazi and did their best to sabotage the French war effort, nor the common people, who were just as likely to follow mountebanks like Doriot as responsible leaders. Koestler records some fantastic conversations with fellow-victims in the concentration camp, and adds that till then, like most middle-class Socialists and Communists, he had never made contact with real proletarians, only with the educated minority. He draws the pessimistic conclusion: "Without education of the masses, no social progress; without social progress, no education of the masses." In *The Scum of the Earth* Koestler ceases to idealise the common people. He has abandoned Stalinism, but he is not a Trotskyist either. This is the book's real link with *Arrival and Departure*, in which what is normally called a revolutionary outlook is dropped, perhaps for good.

*Arrival and Departure* is not a satisfactory book. The pretence that it is a novel is very thin; in effect it is a tract purporting to show that revolutionary creeds are rationalisations of neurotic impulses. With all too neat a symmetry, the book begins and ends with the same action—a leap into a foreign country. A young ex-Communist who has made his escape from Hungary jumps ashore in Portugal, where he hopes to enter the service of Britain, at that time the only power fighting against Germany. His enthusiasm is somewhat cooled by the fact that the British consulate is uninterested in him and almost ignores him for a period of several months, during which his money runs out and other astuter refugees escape to America. He is successively tempted by the World in the form of a Nazi propagandist, the Flesh in the form of a French girl, and —after a nervous breakdown—the Devil in the form of a psycho-analyst. The psycho-analyst drags out of him the fact that his revolutionary enthusiasm is not founded on any real belief in historical necessity, but on a morbid guilt complex arising from an attempt in early childhood to blind his baby brother. By the time that he gets an opportunity of serving the Allies he has lost all reason for wanting to do so, and he is on the point of leaving for America when his irrational impulses seize hold of him again. In practice he cannot abandon the struggle. When the book ends, he is floating down in a parachute over the dark landscape of his native country, where he will be employed as a secret agent of Britain.

As a political statement (and the book is not much more), this is insufficient. Of course it is true in many cases, and it may be true in all cases, that revolutionary activity is the result of personal maladjustment. Those who struggle against society are, on the whole, those who have reason to dislike it, and normal healthy people are no more attracted by violence and illegality than they are by war. The young Nazi in *Arrival and Departure* makes the penetrating remark that one can see what is wrong with the left-wing movement by the ugliness of its women. But after all, this does not invalidate the Socialist case. Actions have results, irrespective of their motives. Marx's ultimate motives may well have been envy and spite, but this does not prove that his conclusions were false. In making the hero of *Arrival and Departure* take his final decision from

a mere instinct not to shirk action and danger, Koestler is
making him suffer a sudden loss of intelligence. With such
a history as he has behind him, he would be able to see that
certain things have to be done, whether our reasons for
doing them are "good" or "bad." History has to move in
a certain direction, even if it has to be pushed that way
by neurotics. In *Arrival and Departure* Peter's idols are
overthrown one after the other. The Russian Revolution
has degenerated, Britain, symbolised by the aged consul
with gouty fingers, is no better, the international class-
conscious proletariat is a myth. But the conclusion (since,
after all, Koestler and his hero "support" the war) ought
to be that getting rid of Hitler is still a worth-while objective, a necessary bit of scavenging in which motives are
almost irrelevant.

To take a rational political decision one must have a
picture of the future. At present Koestler seems to have
none, or rather to have two which cancel out. As an ultimate objective he believes in the Earthly Paradise, the
Sun State which the gladiators set out to establish, and
which has haunted the imagination of Socialists, anarchists and religious heretics for hundreds of years. But
his intelligence tells him that the Earthly Paradise is re-
ceding into the far distance and that what is actually
ahead of us is bloodshed, tyranny and privation. Recently
he described himself as a "short-term pessimist." Every
kind of horror is blowing up over the horizon, but somehow it will all come right in the end. This outlook is probably gaining ground among thinking people: it results
from the very great difficulty, once one has abandoned

orthodox religious belief, of accepting life on earth as inherently miserable, and on the other hand, from the realisation that to make life liveable is a much bigger problem than it recently seemed. Since about 1930 the world has given no reason for optimism whatever. Nothing is in sight except a welter of lies, hatred, cruelty and ignorance, and beyond our present troubles loom vaster ones which are only now entering into the European consciousness. It is quite possible that man's major problems will *never* be solved. But it is also unthinkable! Who is there who dares to look at the world of to-day and say to himself, "It will always be like this: even in a million years it cannot get appreciably better"? So you get the quasi-mystical belief that for the present there is no remedy, all political action is useless, but that somehow, somewhere in space and time, human life will cease to be the miserable brutish thing it now is.

The only easy way out is that of the religious believer, who regards this life merely as a preparation for the next. But few thinking people now believe in life after death, and the number of those who do is probably diminishing. The Christian churches would probably not survive on their own merits if their economic basis were destroyed. The real problem is how to restore the religious attitude while accepting death as final. Men can only be happy when they do not assume that the object of life is happiness. It is most unlikely, however, that Koestler would accept this. There is a well-marked hedonistic strain in his writings, and his failure to find a political position after breaking with Stalinism is a result of this.

The Russian Revolution, the central event in Koestler's life, started out with high hopes. We forget these things now, but a quarter of a century ago it was confidently expected that the Russian Revolution would lead to Utopia. Obviously this has not happened. Koestler is too acute not to see this, and too sensitive not to remember the original objective. Moreover, from his European angle he can see such things as purges and mass deportations for what they are; he is not, like Shaw or Laski, looking at them through the wrong end of the telescope. Therefore he draws the conclusion: This is what revolutions lead to. There is nothing for it except to be a "short-term pessimist," *i.e.* to keep out of politics, make a sort of oasis within which you and your friends can remain sane, and hope that somehow things will be better in a hundred years. At the basis of this lies his hedonism, which leads him to think of the Earthly Paradise as desirable. Perhaps, however, whether desirable or not, it isn't possible. Perhaps some degree of suffering is ineradicable from human life, perhaps the choice before man is always a choice of evils, perhaps even the aim of Socialism is not to make the world perfect but to make it better. All revolutions are failures, but they are not all the same failure. It is his unwillingness to admit this that has led Koestler's mind temporarily into a blind alley and that makes *Arrival and Departure* seem shallow compared with the earlier books. 1944.

# RAFFLES
## AND MISS BLANDISH

NEARLY half a century after his first appearance, Raffles, "the amateur cracksman," is still one of the best-known characters in English fiction. Very few people would need telling that he played cricket for England, had bachelor chambers in the Albany and burgled the Mayfair houses which he also entered as a guest. Just for that reason he and his exploits make a suitable background against which to examine a more modern crime story such as *No Orchids for Miss Blandish*. Any such choice is necessarily arbitrary—I might equally well have chosen *Arsene Lupin*, for instance—but at any rate *No Orchids* and the Raffles books [1] have the common quality of being crime stories which play the limelight on the crim-

[1] *Raffles, A Thief in the Night* and *Mr. Justice Raffles*, by E. W. Hornung. The third of these is definitely a failure, and only the first has the true Raffles atmosphere. Hornung wrote a number of crime stories, usually with a tendency to take the side of the criminal. A successful book in rather the same vein as *Raffles* is *Stingaree*.

inal rather than the policeman. For sociological purposes
they can be compared. *No Orchids* is the 1939 version of
glamorised crime, *Raffles* the 1900 version. What I am
concerned with here is the immense difference in moral
atmosphere between the two books, and the change in the
popular attitude that this probably implies.

At this date, the charm of *Raffles* is partly in the period
atmosphere and partly in the technical excellence of the
stories. Hornung was a very conscientious and on his level
a very able writer. Anyone who cares for sheer efficiency
must admire his work. However, the truly dramatic thing
about Raffles, the thing that makes him a sort of byword
even to this day (only a few weeks ago, in a burglary case,
a magistrate referred to the prisoner as "a Raffles in real
life"), is the fact that he is a *gentleman*. Raffles is presented to us—and this is rubbed home in countless scraps
of dialogue and casual remarks—not as an honest man
who has gone astray, but as a public-school man who has
gone astray. His remorse, when he feels any, is almost
purely social; he has disgraced "the old school," he has
lost his right to enter "decent society," he has forfeited his
amateur status and become a cad. Neither Raffles nor
Bunny appears to feel at all strongly that stealing is
wrong in itself, though Raffles does once justify himself
by the casual remark that "the distribution of property
is all wrong anyway." They think of themselves not as
sinners but as renegades, or simply as outcasts. And the
moral code of most of us is still so close to Raffles' own that
we do feel his situation to be an especially ironical one. A
West End club man who is really a burglar! That is al-

most a story in itself, is it not? But how if it were a plumber or a greengrocer who was really a burglar? Would there be anything inherently dramatic in that? No—although the theme of the "double life," of respectability covering crime, is still there. Even Charles Peace in his clergyman's dog-collar seems somewhat less of a hypocrite than Raffles in his Zingari blazer.

Raffles, of course, is good at all games, but it is peculiarly fitting that his chosen game should be cricket. This allows not only of endless analogies between his cunning as a slow bowler and his cunning as a burglar, but also helps to define the exact nature of his crime. Cricket is not in reality a very popular game in England—it is nowhere near so popular as football, for instance—but it gives expression to a well-marked trait in the English character, the tendency to value "form" or "style" more highly than success. In the eyes of any true cricket-lover it is possible for an innings of ten runs to be "better" (*i.e.* more elegant) than an innings of a hundred runs: cricket is also one of the very few games in which the amateur can excel the professional. It is a game full of forlorn hopes and sudden dramatic changes of fortune, and its rules are so ill-defined that their interpretation is partly an ethical business. When Larwood, for instance, practised body line bowling in Australia he was not actually breaking any rule: he was merely doing something that was "not cricket." Since cricket takes up a lot of time and is rather an expensive game to play, it is predominantly an upperclass game, but for the whole nation it is bound up with such concepts as "good form," "playing the game," etc.,

and it has declined in popularity just as the tradition of
"don't hit a man when he's down" has declined. It is not a
twentieth-century game, and nearly all modern-minded
people dislike it. The Nazis, for instance, were at pains to
discourage cricket, which had gained a certain footing in
Germany before and after the last war. In making Raffles
a cricketer as well as a burglar, Hornung was not merely
providing him with a plausible disguise; he was also drawing the sharpest moral contrast that he was able to imagine.

*Raffles*, no less than *Great Expectations* or *Le Rouge et
le Noir*, is a story of snobbery, and it gains a great deal
from the precariousness of Raffles's social position. A
cruder writer would have made the "gentleman burglar"
a member of the peerage, or at least a baronet. Raffles,
however, is of upper-middle-class origin and is only accepted by the aristocracy because of his personal charm.
"We were in Society but not of it," he says to Bunny towards the end of the book; and "I was asked about for my
cricket." Both he and Bunny accept the values of "Society" unquestionably, and would settle down in it for
good if only they could get away with a big enough haul.
The ruin that constantly threatens them is all the blacker
because they only doubtfully "belong." A duke who has
served a prison sentence is still a duke, whereas a mere
man about town, if once disgraced, ceases to be "about
town" for evermore. The closing chapters of the book,
when Raffles has been exposed and is living under an assumed name, have a twilight of the gods feeling, a mental

atmosphere rather similar to that of Kipling's poem, "Gentleman Rankers":

> "Yes, a trooper of the forces—
> Who has run his own six horses!" etc.

Raffles now belongs irrevocably to the "cohorts of the damned." He can still commit successful burglaries, but there is no way back into Paradise, which means Piccadilly and the M.C.C. According to the public-school code there is only one means of rehabilitation: death in battle. Raffles dies fighting against the Boers (a practised reader would foresee this from the start), and in the eyes of both Bunny and his creator this cancels his crimes.

Both Raffles and Bunny, of course, are devoid of religious belief, and they have no real ethical code, merely certain rules of behaviour which they observe semi-instinctively. But it is just here that the deep moral difference between *Raffles* and *No Orchids* becomes apparent. Raffles and Bunny, after all, are gentlemen, and such standards as they do have are not to be violated. Certain things are "not done," and the idea of doing them hardly arises. Raffles will not, for example, abuse hospitality. He will commit a burglary in a house where he is staying as a guest, but the victim must be a fellow-guest and not the host. He will not commit murder,[1] and he avoids violence

---

[1] 1945. Actually Raffles does kill one man and is more or less consciously responsible for the death of two others. But all three of them are foreigners and have behaved in a very reprehensible manner. He also, on one occasion, contemplates murdering a blackmailer. It is, however, a fairly well-established convention in crime stories that murdering a blackmailer "doesn't count."

wherever possible and prefers to carry out his robberies unarmed. He regards friendship as sacred, and is chivalrous though not moral in his relations with women. He will take extra risks in the name of "sportsmanship," and sometimes even for æsthetic reasons. And above all, he is intensely patriotic. He celebrates the Diamond Jubilee ("For sixty years, Bunny, we've been ruled over by absolutely the finest sovereign the world has ever seen") by despatching to the Queen, through the post, an antique gold cup which he has stolen from the British Museum. He steals, from partly political motives, a pearl which the German Emperor is sending to one of the enemies of Britain, and when the Boer War begins to go badly his one thought is to find his way into the fighting line. At the front he unmasks a spy at the cost of revealing his own identity, and then dies gloriously by a Boer bullet. In this combination of crime and patriotism he resembles his near-contemporary Arsene Lupin, who also scores off the German Emperor and wipes out his very dirty past by enlisting in the Foreign Legion.

It is important to note that by modern standards Raffles's crimes are very petty ones. Four hundred pounds' worth of jewellery seems to him an excellent haul. And though the stories are convincing in their physical detail, they contain very little sensationalism—very few corpses, hardly any blood, no sex crimes, no sadism, no perversions of any kind. It seems to be the case that the crime story, at any rate on its higher levels, has greatly increased in blood-thirstiness during the past twenty years. Some of the early detective stories do not even contain a murder.

The Sherlock Holmes stories, for instance, are not all murders, and some of them do not even deal with an indictable crime. So also with the John Thorndyke stories, while of the Max Carrados stories only a minority are murders. Since 1918, however, a detective story not containing a murder has been a great rarity, and the most disgusting details of dismemberment and exhumation are commonly exploited. Some of the Peter Wimsey stories, for instance, display an extremely morbid interest in corpses. The Raffles stories, written from the angle of the criminal, are much less anti-social than many modern stories written from the angle of the detective. The main impression that they leave behind is of boyishness. They belong to a time when people had standards, though they happened to be foolish standards. Their key-phrase is "not done." The line that they draw between good and evil is as senseless as a Polynesian taboo, but at least, like the taboo, it has the advantage that everyone accepts it.

So much for *Raffles*. Now for a header into the cesspool. *No Orchids for Miss Blandish*, by James Hadley Chase, was published in 1939, but seems to have enjoyed its greatest popularity in 1940, during the Battle of Britain and the blitz. In its main outlines its story is this:

Miss Blandish, the daughter of a millionaire, is kidnapped by some gangsters who are almost immediately surprised and killed off by a larger and better organised gang. They hold her to ransom and extract half a million dollars from her father. Their original plan had been to kill her as soon as the ransom-money was received, but a chance keeps her alive. One of the gang is a young man named Slim, whose sole pleasure in life consists in driving knives into other people's bellies. In childhood he has graduated by cutting up living animals with a pair of rusty scissors. Slim is sexually impotent, but takes a kind of fancy to Miss Blandish. Slim's mother, who is the real brains of the gang, sees in this the chance of curing Slim's impotence, and decides to keep Miss Blandish in custody till Slim shall have succeeded in raping her. After many efforts and much persuasion, including the flogging of Miss Blandish with a length of rubber hosepipe, the rape is achieved. Meanwhile Miss Blandish's father has hired a private detective, and by means of bribery and torture the detective and the police manage to round up and exterminate the whole gang. Slim escapes with Miss Blandish and is killed after a final rape, and the detective prepares to restore Miss Blandish to her family. By this time, however, she has developed such a taste for Slim's caresses [1] that she feels unable to live without him, and she jumps out of the window of a sky-scraper.

Several other points need noticing before one can grasp the full implications of this book. To begin with, its central story bears a very marked resemblance to William Faulkner's novel, *Sanctuary*. Secondly, it is not, as one might expect, the product of an illiterate hack, but a brilliant piece of writing, with hardly a wasted word or a jarring note anywhere. Thirdly, the whole book, *récit* as

[1] 1945. Another reading of the final episode is possible. It may mean merely that Miss Blandish is pregnant. But the interpretation I have given above seems more in keeping with the general brutality of the book.

well as dialogue, is written in the American language; the author, an Englishman who has (I believe) never been in the United States, seems to have made a complete mental transference to the American underworld. Fourthly, the book sold, according to its publishers, no less than half a million copies.

I have already outlined the plot, but the subject-matter is much more sordid and brutal than this suggests. The book contains eight full-dress murders, an unassessable number of casual killings and woundings, an exhumation (with a careful reminder of the stench), the flogging of Miss Blandish, the torture of another woman with red-hot cigarette-ends, a strip-tease act, a third-degree scene of unheard-of cruelty and much else of the same kind. It assumes great sexual sophistication in its readers (there is a scene, for instance, in which a gangster, presumably of masochistic tendency, has an orgasm in the moment of being knifed), and it takes for granted the most complete corruption and self-seeking as the norm of human behaviour. The detective, for instance, is almost as great a rogue as the gangsters, and actuated by nearly the same motives. Like them, he is in pursuit of "five hundred grand." It is necessary to the machinery of the story that Mr. Blandish should be anxious to get his daughter back, but apart from this, such things as affection, friendship, good nature or even ordinary politeness simply do not enter. Nor, to any great extent, does normal sexuality. Ultimately only one motive is at work throughout the whole story: the pursuit of power.

It should be noticed that the book is not in the ordinary

sense pornography. Unlike most books that deal in sexual sadism, it lays the emphasis on the cruelty and not on the pleasure. Slim, the ravisher of Miss Blandish, has "wet, slobbering lips": this is disgusting, and it is meant to be disgusting. But the scenes describing cruelty to women are comparatively perfunctory. The real high-spots of the book are cruelties committed by men upon other men: above all, the third-degreeing of the gangster, Eddie Schultz, who is lashed into a chair and flogged on the windpipe with truncheons, his arms broken by fresh blows as he breaks loose. In another of Mr. Chase's books, *He Won't Need It Now*, the hero, who is intended to be a sympathetic and perhaps even noble character, is described as stamping on somebody's face, and then, having crushed the man's mouth in, grinding his heel round and round in it. Even when physical incidents of this kind are not occurring, the mental atmosphere of these books is always the same. Their whole theme is the struggle for power and the triumph of the strong over the weak. The big gangsters wipe out the little ones as mercilessly as a pike gobbling up the little fish in a pond; the police kill off the criminals as cruelly as the angler kills the pike. If ultimately one sides with the police against the gangsters, it is merely because they are better organised and more powerful, because, in fact, the law is a bigger racket than crime. Might is right: *væ victis*.

As I have mentioned already, *No Orchids* enjoyed its greatest vogue in 1940, though it was successfully running as a play till some time later. It was, in fact, one of the things that helped to console people for the boredom of being bombed. Early in the war the *New Yorker* had a picture of a little man approaching a news-stall littered with papers with such headlines as "Great Tank Battles in Northern France," "Big Naval Battle in the North Sea," "Huge Air Battles over the Channel," etc. etc. The little man is saying, "*Action Stories*, please." That little man stood for all the drugged millions to whom the world of the gangsters and the prize-ring is more "real," more "tough," than such things as wars, revolutions, earthquakes, famines and pestilences. From the point of view of a reader of *Action Stories*, a description of the London blitz, or of the struggles of the European underground parties, would be "sissy stuff." On the other hand, some puny gun-battle in Chicago, resulting in perhaps half a dozen deaths, would seem genuinely "tough." This habit of mind is now extremely widespread. A soldier sprawls in a muddy trench, with the machine-gun bullets crackling a foot or two overhead, and whiles away his intolerable boredom by reading an American gangster story. And what is it that makes that story so exciting? Precisely the fact that people are shooting at each other with machine-guns! Neither the soldier nor anyone else sees anything curious in this. It is taken for granted that an imaginary bullet is more thrilling than a real one.

The obvious explanation is that in real life one is usually a passive victim, whereas in the adventure story one can think of oneself as being at the centre of events. But there is more to it than that. Here it is necessary to refer again to the curious fact of *No Orchids* being written—

with technical errors, perhaps, but certainly with considerable skill—in the American language.

There exists in America an enormous literature of more or less the same stamp as *No Orchids*. Quite apart from books, there is the huge array of "pulp magazines," graded so as to cater to different kinds of fantasy, but nearly all having much the same mental atmosphere. A few of them go in for straight pornography, but the great majority are quite plainly aimed at sadists and masochists. Sold at threepence a copy under the title of Yank Mags,[1] these things used to enjoy considerable popularity in England, but when the supply dried up owing to the war, no satisfactory substitute was forthcoming. English imitations of the "pulp magazine" do now exist, but they are poor things compared with the original. English crook films, again, never approach the American crook film in brutality. And yet the career of Mr. Chase shows how deep the American influence has already gone. Not only is he himself living a continuous fantasy-life in the Chicago underworld, but he can count on hundreds of thousands of readers who know what is meant by a "clipshop" or the "hotsquat," do not have to do mental arithmetic when confronted by "fifty grand," and understand at sight a sentence like "Johnnie was a rummy and only two jumps ahead of the nut-factory." Evidently there are great numbers of English people who are partly Americanised in

[1] They are said to have been imported into this country as ballast, which accounted for their low price and crumpled appearance. Since the war the ships have been ballasted with something more useful, probably gravel.

language and, one ought to add, in moral outlook. For there was no popular protest against *No Orchids*. In the end it was withdrawn, but only retrospectively, when a later work, *Miss Callaghan Comes to Grief*, brought Mr. Chase's books to the attention of the authorities. Judging by casual conversations at the time, ordinary readers got a mild thrill out of the obscenities of *No Orchids*, but saw nothing undesirable in the book as a whole. Many people, incidentally, were under the impression that it was an American book reissued in England.

The thing that the ordinary reader *ought* to have objected to—almost certainly would have objected to, a few decades earlier—was the equivocal attitude towards crime. It is implied throughout *No Orchids* that being a criminal is only reprehensible in the sense that it does not pay. Being a policeman pays better, but there is no moral difference, since the police use essentially criminal methods. In a book like *He Won't Need It Now* the distinction between crime and crime-prevention practically disappears. This is a new departure for English sensational fiction, in which till recently there has always been a sharp distinction between right and wrong and a general agreement that virtue must triumph in the last chapter. English books glorifying crime (modern crime, that is—pirates and highwaymen are different) are very rare. Even a book like *Raffles*, as I have pointed out, is governed by powerful taboos, and it is clearly understood that Raffles's crimes must be expiated sooner or later. In America, both in life and fiction, the tendency to tolerate crime, even to admire the criminal so long as he is successful, is very

much more marked. It is, indeed, ultimately this attitude
that has made it possible for crime to flourish upon so
huge a scale. Books have been written about Al Capone
that are hardly different in tone from the books written
about Henry Ford, Stalin, Lord Northcliffe and all the
rest of the "log cabin to White House" brigade. And
switching back eighty years, one finds Mark Twain
adopting much the same attitude towards the disgusting
bandit Slade, hero of twenty-eight murders, and towards
the Western desperadoes generally. They were successful,
they "made good," therefore he admired them.

In a book like *No Orchids* one is not, as in the old-style
crime story, simply escaping from dull reality into an imaginary world of action. One's escape is essentially into
cruelty and sexual perversion. *No Orchids* is aimed at the
power-instinct, which *Raffles* or the Sherlock Holmes stories are not. At the same time the English attitude towards
crime is not so superior to the American as I may have
seemed to imply. It too is mixed up with power-worship,
and has become more noticeably so in the last twenty
years. A writer who is worth examining is Edgar Wallace,
especially in such typical books as *The Orator* and the
Mr. J. G. Reeder stories. Wallace was one of the first
crime-story writers to break away from the old tradition
of the private detective and make his central figure a
Scotland Yard official. Sherlock Holmes is an amateur,
solving his problems without the help and even, in the
earlier stories, against the opposition of the police. Moreover, like Lupin, he is essentially an intellectual, even a
scientist. He reasons logically from observed fact, and his

intellectuality is constantly contrasted with the routine methods of the police. Wallace objected strongly to this slur, as he considered it, on Scotland Yard, and in several newspaper articles he went out of his way to denounce Holmes by name. His own ideal was the detective inspector who catches criminals not because he is intellectually brilliant but because he is part of an all-powerful organisation. Hence the curious fact that in Wallace's most characteristic stories the "clue" and the "deduction" play no part. The criminal is always defeated either by an incredible coincidence, or because in some unexplained manner the police know all about the crime beforehand. The tone of the stories makes it quite clear that Wallace's admiration for the police is pure bully-worship. A Scotland Yard detective is the most powerful kind of being that he can imagine, while the criminal figures in his mind as an outlaw against whom anything is permissible, like the condemned slaves in the Roman arena. His policemen behave much more brutally than British policeman do in real life —they hit people without provocation, fire revolvers past their ears to terrify them and so on—and some of the stories exhibit a fearful intellectual sadism. (For instance, Wallace likes to arrange things so that the villain is hanged on the same day as the heroine is married.) But it is sadism after the English fashion: that is to say, it is unconscious, there is not overtly any sex in it, and it keeps within the bounds of the law. The British public tolerates a harsh criminal law and gets a kick out of monstrously unfair murder trials: but still this is better, on any count, than tolerating or admiring crime. If one must worship a

bully, it is better that he should be a policeman than a
gangster. Wallace is still governed to some extent by the
concept of "not done." In *No Orchids* anything is "done"
so long as it leads on to power. All the barriers are down,
all the motives are out in the open. Chase is a worse symptom than Wallace, to the extent that all-in wrestling is
worse than boxing, or Fascism is worse than capitalist democracy.

In borrowing from William Faulkner's *Sanctuary*,
Chase only took the plot; the mental atmosphere of the
two books is not similar. Chase really derives from other
sources, and this particular bit of borrowing is only sym-
bolic. What it symbolises is the vulgarisation of ideas
which is constantly happening, and which probably happens faster in an age of print. Chase has been described
as "Faulkner for the masses," but it would be more accurate to describe him as Carlyle for the masses. He is a
popular writer—there are many such in America, but they
are still rarities in England—who has caught up with
what it is now fashionable to call "realism," meaning the
doctrine that might is right. The growth of "realism" has
been the great feature of the intellectual history of our
own age. Why this should be so is a complicated question.
The interconnection between sadism, masochism, success-
worship, power-worship, nationalism and totalitarianism
is a huge subject whose edges have barely been scratched,
and even to mention it is considered somewhat indelicate.
To take merely the first example that comes to mind, I
believe no one has ever pointed out the sadistic and masochistic element in Bernard Shaw's work, still less sug-

gested that this probably has some connection with Shaw's admiration for dictators. Fascism is often loosely equated with sadism, but nearly always by people who see nothing wrong in the most slavish worship of Stalin. The truth is, of course, that the countless English intellectuals who kiss the arse of Stalin are not different from the minority who give their allegiance to Hitler or Mussolini, nor from the efficiency experts who preached "punch," "drive," "personality" and "learn to be a Tiger man" in the nineteen-twenties, nor from that older generation of intellectuals, Carlyle, Creasey and the rest of them, who bowed down before German militarism. All of them are worshipping power and successful cruelty. It is important to notice that the cult of power tends to be mixed up with a love of cruelty and wickedness *for their own sakes*. A tyrant is all the more admired if he happens to be a bloodstained crook as well, and "the end justifies the means" often becomes, in effect, "the means justify themselves provided they are dirty enough." This idea colours the outlook of all sympathisers with totalitarianism, and accounts, for instance, for the positive delight with which many English intellectuals greeted the Nazi-Soviet pact. It was a step only doubtfully useful to the U.S.S.R., but it was entirely unmoral, and for that reason to be admired; the explanations of it, which were numerous and self-contradictory, could come afterwards.

Until recently the characteristic adventure stories of the English-speaking peoples have been stories in which the hero fights *against odds*. This is true all the way from Robin Hood to Pop-eye the Sailor. Perhaps the basic myth of the Western world is Jack the Giant-killer, but to be brought up to date this should be renamed Jack the Dwarf-killer, and there already exists considerable literature which teaches, either overtly or implicitly, that one should side with the big man against the little man. Most of what is now written about foreign policy is simply an embroidery on this theme, and for several decades such phrases as "Play the game," "Don't hit a man when he's down" and "It's not cricket" have never failed to draw a snigger from anyone of intellectual pretensions. What is comparatively new is to find the accepted pattern according to which (*a*) right is right and wrong is wrong, whoever wins, and (*b*) weakness must be respected, disappearing from popular literature as well. When I first read D. H. Lawrence's novels, at the age of about twenty, I was puzzled by the fact that there did not seem to be any classification of the characters into "good" and "bad." Lawrence seemed to sympathise with all of them about equally and this was so unusual as to give me the feeling of having lost my bearings. To-day no one would think of looking for heroes and villains in a serious novel, but in lowbrow fiction one still expects to find a sharp distinction between right and wrong and between legality and illegality. The common people, on the whole, are still living in the world of absolute good and evil from which the intellectuals have long since escaped. But the popularity of *No Orchids* and the American books and magazines to which it is akin shows how rapidly the doctrine of "realism" is gaining ground.

Several people, after reading *No Orchids*, have remarked

to me, "It's pure Fascism." This is a correct description, although the book has not the smallest connection with politics and very little with social or economic problems. It has merely the same relation to Fascism as, say, Trollope's novels have to nineteenth-century capitalism. It is a day dream appropriate to a totalitarian age. In his imagined world of gangsters Chase is presenting, as it were, a distilled version of the modern political scene, in which such things as mass bombing of civilians, the use of hostages, torture to obtain confessions, secret prisons, execution without trial, floggings with rubber truncheons, drownings in cesspools, systematic falsification of records and statistics, treachery, bribery and quislingism are normal and morally neutral, even admirable when they are done in a large and bold way. The average man is not directly interested in politics, and when he reads, he wants the current struggles of the world to be translated into a simple story about individuals. He can take an interest in Slim and Fenner as he could not in the G.P.U. and the Gestapo. People worship power in the form in which they are able to understand it. A twelve-year-old boy worships Jack Dempsey. An adolescent in a Glasgow slum worships Al Capone. An aspiring pupil at a business college worships Lord Nuffield. A *New Statesman* reader worships Stalin. There is a difference in intellectual maturity, but none in moral outlook. Thirty years ago the heroes of popular fiction had nothing in common with Mr. Chase's gangsters and detectives, and the idols of the English liberal intelligentsia were also comparatively sympathetic figures. Between Holmes and Fenner on the one hand, and between Abraham Lincoln and Stalin on the other, there is a similar gulf.

One ought not to infer too much from the success of Mr. Chase's books. It is possible that it is an isolated phenomenon, brought about by the mingled boredom and brutality of war. But if such books should definitely acclimatise themselves in England, instead of being merely a half-understood import from America, there would be good grounds for dismay. In choosing *Raffles* as a background for *No Orchids* I deliberately chose a book which by the standards of its time was morally equivocal. Raffles, as I have pointed out, has no real moral code, no religion, certainly no social consciousness. All he has is a set of reflexes —the nervous system, as it were, of a gentleman. Give him a sharp tap on this reflex or that (they are called "sport," "pal," "woman," "king and country" and so forth), and you get a predictable reaction. In Mr. Chase's books there are no gentlemen and no taboos. Emancipation is complete, Freud and Machiavelli have reached the outer suburbs. Comparing the schoolboy atmosphere of the one book with the cruelty and corruption of the other, one is driven to feel that snobbishness, like hypocrisy, is a check upon behaviour whose value from a social point of view has been underrated.                     **1944.**

# IN DEFENCE
## OF P. G. WODEHOUSE

WHEN the Germans made their rapid advance through Belgium in the early summer of 1940, they captured, among other things, Mr. P. G. Wodehouse, who had been living throughout the early part of the war in his villa at Le Touquet, and seems not to have realised until the last moment that he was in any danger. As he was led away into captivity, he is said to have remarked, "Perhaps after this I shall write a serious book." He was placed for the time being under house arrest, and from his subsequent statements it appears that he was treated in a fairly friendly way, German officers in the neighbourhood frequently "dropping in for a bath or a party."

Over a year later, on 25th June 1941, the news came that Wodehouse had been released from internment and was living at the Adlon Hotel in Berlin. On the following day the public was astonished to learn that he had agreed to do some broadcasts of a "non-political" nature over the German radio. The full texts of these broadcasts are not easy to obtain at this date, but Wodehouse seems to have

done five of them between 26th June and 2nd July, when
the Germans took him off the air again. The first broadcast, on 26th June, was not made on the Nazi radio but
took the form of an interview with Harry Flannery, the
representative of the Columbia Broadcasting System,
which still had its correspondents in Berlin. Wodehouse
also published in the *Saturday Evening Post* an article
which he had written while still in the internment camp.

The article and the broadcasts dealt mainly with Wodehouse's experiences in internment, but they did include a
very few comments on the war. The following are fair
samples:

> "I never was interested in politics. I'm quite un-
> able to work up any kind of belligerent feeling. Just
> as I'm about to feel belligerent about some country I
> meet a decent sort of chap. We go out together and
> lose any fighting thoughts or feelings."
>
> "A short time ago they had a look at me on parade
> and got the right idea; at least they sent us to the
> local lunatic asylum. And I have been there forty-
> two weeks. There is a good deal to be said for intern-
> ment. It keeps you out of the saloon and helps you to
> keep up with your reading. The chief trouble is that
> it means you are away from home for a long time.
> When I join my wife I had better take along a letter
> of introduction to be on the safe side."
>
> "In the days before the war I had always been
> modestly proud of being an Englishman, but now
> that I have been some months resident in this bin or

repository of Englishmen I am not so sure. . . . The only concession I want from Germany is that she gives me a loaf of bread, tells the gentlemen with muskets at the main gate to look the other way, and leaves the rest to me. In return I am prepared to hand over India, an autographed set of my books, and to reveal the secret process of cooking sliced potatoes on a radiator. This offer holds good till Wednesday week."

The first extract quoted above caused great offence. Wodehouse was also censured for using (in the interview with Flannery) the phrase "whether Britain wins the war or not," and he did not make things better by describing in another broadcast the filthy habits of some Belgian prisoners among whom he was interned. The Germans recorded this broadcast and repeated it a number of times. They seem to have supervised his talks very lightly, and they allowed him not only to be funny about the discomforts of internment but to remark that "the internees at Trost camp all fervently believe that Britain will eventually win." The general upshot of the talks, however, was that he had not been ill treated and bore no malice.

These broadcasts caused an immediate uproar in England. There were questions in Parliament, angry editorial comments in the press, and a stream of letters from fellow-authors, nearly all of them disapproving, though one or two suggested that it would be better to suspend judgment, and several pleaded that Wodehouse probably did not realise what he was doing. On 15th July, the Home

Service of the B.B.C. carried an extremely violent Post-script by "Cassandra" of the *Daily Mirror*, accusing Wodehouse of "selling his country." This postscript made free use of such expressions as "Quisling" and "worship-ping the Führer." The main charge was that Wodehouse had agreed to do German propaganda as a way of buying himself out of the internment camp.

"Cassandra's" Postscript caused a certain amount of protest, but on the whole it seems to have intensified popu-lar feeling against Wodehouse. One result of it was that numerous lending libraries withdrew Wodehouse's books from circulation. Here is a typical news item:

> "Within twenty-four hours of listening to the broadcast of Cassandra, the *Daily Mirror* columnist, Portadown (North Ireland) Urban District Council banned P. G. Wodehouse's books from their public library. Mr. Edward McCann said that Cassandra's broadcast had clinched the matter. Wodehouse was funny no longer." (*Daily Mirror.*)

In addition the B.B.C. banned Wodehouse's lyrics from the air and was still doing so a couple of years later. As late as December 1944 there were demands in Parliament that Wodehouse should be put on trial as a traitor.

There is an old saying that if you throw enough mud some of it will stick, and the mud has stuck to Wodehouse in a rather peculiar way. An impression has been left be-hind that Wodehouse's talks (not that anyone remembers what he said in them) showed him up not merely as a traitor but as an ideological sympathiser with Fascism.

Even at the time several letters to the press claimed that "Fascist tendencies" could be detected in his books, and the charge has been repeated since. I shall try to analyse the mental atmosphere of those books in a moment, but it is important to realise that the events of 1941 do not convict Wodehouse of anything worse than stupidity. The really interesting question is how and why he could be so stupid. When Flannery met Wodehouse (released, but still under guard) at the Adlon Hotel in June 1941, he saw at once that he was dealing with a political innocent, and when preparing him for their broadcast interview he had to warn him against making some exceedingly unfortunate remarks, one of which was by implication slightly anti-Russian. As it was, the phrase "whether England wins or not" did get through. Soon after the interview Wodehouse told him that he was also going to broadcast on the Nazi radio, apparently not realising that this action had any special significance. Flannery comments:[1]

> "By this time the Wodehouse plot was evident. It was one of the best Nazi publicity stunts of the war, the first with a human angle. . . . Plack (Goebbels's assistant) had gone to the camp near Gleiwitz to see Wodehouse, found that the author was completely without political sense, and had an idea. He suggested to Wodehouse that in return for being released from the prison camp he write a series of broadcasts about his experiences; there would be no censorship

[1] *Assignment to Berlin,* by Harry W. Flannery. (Alfred A. Knopf, 1942.)

and he would put them on the air himself. In making that proposal Plack showed that he knew his man. He knew that Wodehouse made fun of the English in all his stories and that he seldom wrote in any other way, that he was still living in the period about which he wrote and had no conception of Nazism and all it meant. Wodehouse was his own Bertie Wooster."

The striking of an actual bargain between Wodehouse and Plack seems to be merely Flannery's own interpretation. The arrangement may have been of a much less definite kind, and to judge from the broadcasts themselves, Wodehouse's main idea in making them was to keep in touch with his public and—the comedian's ruling passion —to get a laugh. Obviously they are not the utterances of a Quisling of the type of Ezra Pound or John Amery, nor, probably, of a person capable of understanding the nature of Quislingism. Flannery seems to have warned Wodehouse that it would be unwise to broadcast, but not very forcibly. He adds that Wodehouse (though in one broadcast he refers to himself as an Englishman) seemed to regard himself as an American citizen. He had contemplated naturalisation, but had never filled in the necessary papers. He even used, to Flannery, the phrase, "We're not at war with Germany."

I have before me a bibliography of P. G. Wodehouse's works. It names round about fifty books, but is certainly incomplete. It is as well to be honest, and I ought to start by admitting that there are many books by Wodehouse— perhaps a quarter or a third of the total—which I have not read. It is not, indeed, easy to read the whole output of a popular writer who is normally published in cheap editions. But I have followed his work fairly closely since 1911, when I was eight years old, and am well acquainted with its peculiar mental atmosphere—an atmosphere which has not, of course, remained completely unchanged, but shows little alteration since about 1925. In the passage from Flannery's book which I quoted above there are two remarks which would immediately strike any attentive reader of Wodehouse. One is to the effect that Wodehouse "was still living in the period about which he wrote," and the other that the Nazi Propaganda Ministry made use of him because he "made fun of the English." The second statement is based on a misconception to which I will return presently. But Flannery's other comment is quite true and contains in it part of the clue to Wodehouse's behaviour.

A thing that people often forget about P. G. Wodehouse's novels is how long ago the better-known of them were written. We think of him as in some sense typifying the silliness of the nineteen-twenties and nineteen-thirties, but in fact the scenes and characters by which he is best remembered had all made their appearance before 1925. Psmith first appeared in 1909, having been foreshadowed by other characters in earlier school-stories. Blandings Castle, with Baxter and the Earl of Emsworth both in residence, was introduced in 1915. The Jeeves-Wooster cycle began in 1919, both Jeeves and Wooster having made brief appearances earlier. Ukridge appeared in 1924. When one looks through the list of Wodehouse's books from 1902 onwards, one can observe three fairly well-marked periods. The first is the school-story period. It includes such books as *The Gold Bat, The Pothunters,* etc., and has its high-spot in *Mike* (1909). *Psmith in the City,* published in the following year, belongs in this category, though it is not directly concerned with school life. The next is the American period. Wodehouse seems to have lived in the United States from about 1913 to 1920, and for a while showed signs of becoming Americanised in idiom and outlook. Some of the stories in *The Man with Two Left Feet* (1917) appear to have been influenced by O. Henry, and other books written about this time contain Americanisms (*e.g.* "highball" for "whisky and soda") which an Englishman would not normally use *in propria persona.* Nevertheless, almost all the books of this period —*Psmith, Journalist; The Little Nugget; The Indiscretions of Archie; Piccadilly Jim* and various others—depend for their effect on the *contrast* between English and American manners. English characters appear in an American setting, or *vice versa*: there is a certain number of purely English stories, but hardly any purely American ones. The third period might fitly be called the country-house period. By the early nineteen-twenties Wodehouse must have been making a very large income, and the social status of his characters moved upwards accordingly, though the Ukridge stories form a partial exception. The typical setting is now a country mansion, a luxurious bachelor flat or an expensive golf club. The schoolboy athleticism of the earlier books fades out, cricket and football giving way to golf, and the element of farce and burlesque becomes more marked. No doubt many of the later books, such as *Summer Lightning*, are light comedy rather than pure farce, but the occasional attempts at moral earnestness which can be found in *Psmith, Journalist*; *The Little Nugget*; *The Coming of Bill*; *The Man with Two Left Feet* and some of the school stories, no longer appear. Mike Jackson has turned into Bertie Wooster. That, however, is not a very startling metamorphosis, and one of the most noticeable things about Wodehouse is his *lack* of development. Books like *The Gold Bat* and *Tales of St. Austin's*, written in the opening years of this century, already have the familiar atmosphere. How much of a formula the writing of his later books had become one can see from the fact that he continued to write stories of English life although throughout the sixteen years before his internment he was living at Hollywood and Le Touquet.

*Mike*, which is now a difficult book to obtain in an unabridged form, must be one of the best "light" school stories in English. But though its incidents are largely farcical, it is by no means a satire on the public-school system, and *The Gold Bat, The Pothunters*, etc., are even less so. Wodehouse was educated at Dulwich, and then worked in a bank and graduated into novel-writing by way of very cheap journalism. It is clear that for many years he remained "fixated" on his old school and loathed the unromantic job and the lower-middle-class surroundings in which he found himself. In the early stories the "glamour" of public-school life (house matches, fagging, teas round the study fire, etc.) is laid on fairly thick, and the "play the game" code of morals is accepted with not many reservations. Wrykyn, Wodehouse's imaginary public school, is a school of a more fashionable type than Dulwich, and one gets the impression that between *The Gold Bat* (1904) and *Mike* (1909) Wrykyn itself has become more expensive and moved farther from London. Psychologically the most revealing book of Wodehouse's early period is *Psmith in the City*. Mike Jackson's father has suddenly lost his money, and Mike, like Wodehouse himself, is thrust at the age of about eighteen into an ill-paid subordinate job in a bank. Psmith is similarly employed, though not from financial necessity. Both this book and *Psmith, Journalist* (1915) are unusual in that they display a certain amount of political consciousness. Psmith at this stage chooses to call himself a Socialist—in his mind, and no doubt in Wodehouse's, this means no more than ignoring class distinctions—and on one occasion the two boys attend an open-air meeting on Clapham Common and go home to tea with an elderly Socialist orator, whose shabby-genteel home is described with some accuracy. But the most striking feature of the book is Mike's inability to wean himself from the atmosphere of school. He enters upon his job without any pretence of enthusiasm, and his main desire is not, as one might expect, to find a more interesting and useful job, but simply to be playing cricket. When he has to find himself lodgings he chooses to settle at Dulwich, because there he will be near a school and will be able to hear the agreeable sound of the ball striking against the bat. The climax of the book comes when Mike gets the chance to play in a county match and simply

walks out of his job in order to do so. The point is that
Wodehouse here sympathises with Mike: indeed he identifies himself with him, for it is clear enough that Mike
bears the same relation to Wodehouse as Julien Sorel to
Stendhal. But he created many other heroes essentially
similar. Through the books of this and the next period
there passes a whole series of young men to whom playing
games and "keeping fit" are a sufficient life-work. Wodehouse is almost incapable of imagining a desirable job.
The great thing is to have money of your own, or, failing
that, to find a sinecure. The hero of *Something Fresh*
(1915) escapes from low-class journalism by becoming
physical-training instructor to a dyspeptic millionaire:
this is regarded as a step up, morally as well as financially.

In the books of the third period there is no narcissism
and no serious interludes, but the implied moral and social
background has changed much less than might appear at
first sight. If one compares Bertie Wooster with Mike, or
even with the rugger-playing prefects of the earliest
school stories, one sees that the only real difference between them is that Bertie is richer and lazier. His ideals
would be almost the same as theirs, but he fails to live up
to them. Archie Moffam, in *The Indiscretions of Archie*
(1921), is a type intermediate between Bertie and the
earlier heroes: he is an ass, but he is also honest, kind-
hearted, athletic and courageous. From first to last Wodehouse takes the public-school code of behaviour for
granted, with the difference that in his later, more sophisticated period he prefers to show his characters violating
it or living up to it against their will:

"Bertie! You wouldn't let down a pal?"

"Yes, I would."

"But we were at school together, Bertie."

"I don't care."

"The old school, Bertie, the old school!"

"Oh, well—dash it!"

Bertie, a sluggish Don Quixote, has no wish to tilt at windmills, but he would hardly think of refusing to do so when honour calls. Most of the people whom Wodehouse intends as sympathetic characters are parasites, and some of them are plain imbeciles, but very few of them could be described as immoral. Even Ukridge is a visionary rather than a plain crook. The most immoral, or rather un-moral, of Wodehouse's characters is Jeeves, who acts as a foil to Bertie Wooster's comparative high-mindedness and perhaps symbolises the widespread English belief that intelligence and unscrupulousness are much the same thing. How closely Wodehouse sticks to conventional morality can be seen from the fact that nowhere in his books is there anything in the nature of a sex joke. This is an enormous sacrifice for a farcical writer to make. Not only are there no dirty jokes, but there are hardly any compromising situations: the horns-on-the-forehead motif is almost completely avoided. Most of the full-length books, of course, contain a "love interest," but it is always at the light-comedy level: the love affair, with its complications and its idyllic scenes, goes on and on, but, as the saying goes, "nothing happens." It is significant that Wodehouse, by nature a writer of farces, was able to collaborate more than once with Ian Hay, a serio-comic writer and an exponent (vide *Pip*, etc.) of the "clean-living Englishman" tradition at its silliest.

In *Something Fresh* Wodehouse had discovered the comic possibilities of the English aristocracy, and a succession of ridiculous but, save in a very few instances, not actually contemptible barons, earls and what-not followed accordingly. This had the rather curious effect of causing Wodehouse to be regarded, outside England, as a penetrating satirist of English society. Hence Flannery's statement that Wodehouse "made fun of the English," which is the impression he would probably make on a German or even an American reader. Some time after the broadcasts from Berlin I was discussing them with a young Indian Nationalist who defended Wodehouse warmly. He took it for granted that Wodehouse *had* gone over to the enemy, which from his own point of view was the right thing to do. But what interested me was to find that he regarded Wodehouse as an anti-British writer who had done useful work by showing up the British aristocracy in their true colours. This is a mistake that it would be very difficult for an English person to make, and is a good instance of the way in which books, especially humorous books, lose their finer nuances when they reach a foreign audience. For it is clear enough that Wodehouse is *not* anti-British, and not anti-upper class either. On the contrary, a harmless old-fashioned snobbishness is perceptible all through his work. Just as an intelligent Catholic is able to see that the blasphemies of Baudelaire or James Joyce are not seriously damaging to the Catholic faith, so an

English reader can see that in creating such characters as
Hildebrand Spencer Poyns de Burgh John Hanneyside
Coombe-Crombie, 12th Earl of Dreever, Wodehouse is not
really attacking the social hierarchy. Indeed, no one who
genuinely despised titles would write of them so much.
Wodehouse's attitude towards the English social system
is the same as his attitude towards the public-school moral
code—a mild facetiousness covering an unthinking acceptance. The Earl of Emsworth is funny because an earl
ought to have more dignity, and Bertie Wooster's helpless
dependence on Jeeves is funny partly because the servant
ought not to be superior to the master. An American
reader can mistake these two, and others like them, for
hostile caricatures, because he is inclined to be Anglophobe
already and they correspond to his preconceived ideas
about a decadent aristocracy. Bertie Wooster, with his
spats and his cane, is the traditional stage Englishman.
But, as any English reader would see, Wodehouse intends
him as a sympathetic figure, and Wodehouse's real sin has
been to present the English upper classes as much nicer
people than they are. All through his books certain problems are constantly avoided. Almost without exception his
moneyed young men are unassuming, good mixers, not
avaricious: their tone is set for them by Psmith, who re-
tains his own upper-class exterior but bridges the social
gap by addressing everyone as "Comrade."

But there is another important point about Bertie
Wooster: his out-of-dateness. Conceived in 1917 or there-
abouts, Bertie really belongs to an epoch earlier than that.
He is the "knut" of the pre-1914 period, celebrated in

such songs as "Gilbert the Filbert" or "Reckless Reggie of the Regent's Palace." The kind of life that Wodehouse writes about by preference, the life of the "clubman" or "man about town," the elegant young man who lounges all the morning in Piccadilly with a cane under his arm and a carnation in his buttonhole, barely survived into the nineteen-twenties. It is significant that Wodehouse could publish in 1936 a book entitled *Young Men in Spats*. For who was wearing spats at that date? They had gone out of fashion quite ten years earlier. But the traditional "knut," the "Piccadilly Johnny," *ought* to wear spats, just as the pantomime Chinese ought to wear a pigtail. A humorous writer is not obliged to keep up to date, and having struck one or two good veins, Wodehouse continued to exploit them with a regularity that was no doubt all the easier because he did not set foot in England during the sixteen years that preceded his internment. His picture of English society had been formed before 1914, and it was a naïve, traditional and, at bottom, admiring picture. Nor did he ever become genuinely Americanised. As I have pointed out, spontaneous Americanisms do occur in the books of the middle period, but Wodehouse remained English enough to find American slang an amusing and slightly shocking novelty. He loves to thrust a slang phrase or a crude fact in among Wardour Street English ("With a hollow groan Ukridge borrowed five shillings from me and went out into the night"), and expressions like "a piece of cheese" or "bust him on the noggin" lend themselves to this purpose. But the trick had been developed before he made any American contacts, and his use of garbled quotations is a common device of English writers running back to Fielding. As Mr. John Hayward has pointed out,[1] Wodehouse owes a good deal to his knowledge of English literature and especially of Shakespeare. His books are aimed, not, obviously, at a highbrow audience, but at an audience educated along traditional lines. When, for instance, he describes somebody as heaving "the kind of sigh that Prometheus might have heaved when the vulture dropped in for its lunch," he is assuming that his readers will know something of Greek mythology. In his early days the writers he admired were probably Barry Pain, Jerome K. Jerome, W. W. Jacobs, Kipling and F. Anstey, and he has remained closer to them than to the quick-moving American comic writers such as Ring Lardner or Damon Runyon. In his radio interview with Flannery, Wodehouse wondered whether "the kind of people and the kind of England I write about will live after the war," not realising that they were ghosts already. "He was still living in the period about which he wrote," says Flannery, meaning, probably, the nineteen-twenties. But the period was really the Edwardian age, and Bertie Wooster, if he ever existed, was killed round about 1915.

If my analysis of Wodehouse's mentality is accepted, the idea that in 1941 he consciously aided the Nazi propaganda machine becomes untenable and even ridiculous. He *may* have been induced to broadcast by the promise of an earlier release (he was due for release a few months later,

[1] *P. G. Wodehouse,* by John Hayward. (*The Saturday Book,* 1942.) I believe this is the only full-length critical essay on Wodehouse.

on reaching his sixtieth birthday), but he cannot have realised that what he did would be damaging to British interests. As I have tried to show, his moral outlook has remained that of a public-school boy, and according to the public-school code, treachery in time of war is the most unforgivable of all the sins. But how could he fail to grasp that what he did would be a big propaganda score for the Germans and would bring down a torrent of disapproval on his own head? To answer this one must take two things into consideration. First, Wodehouse's complete lack—so far as one can judge from his printed works—of political awareness. It is nonsense to talk of "Fascist tendencies" in his books. There are no post-1918 tendencies at all. Throughout his work there is a certain uneasy awareness of the problem of class distinctions, and scattered through it at various dates there are ignorant though not un-friendly references to Socialism. In *The Heart of a Goof* (1926) there is a rather silly story about a Russian novel-ist, which seems to have been inspired by the factional struggle then raging in the U.S.S.R. But the references in it to the Soviet system are entirely frivolous and, consider-ing the date, not markedly hostile. That is about the ex-tent of Wodehouse's political consciousness, so far as it is discoverable from his writings. Nowhere, so far as I know, does he so much as use the word "Fascism" or "Nazism." In left-wing circles, indeed in "enlightened" circles of any kind, to broadcast on the Nazi radio, to have any truck with the Nazis whatever, would have seemed just as shock-ing an action before the war as during it. But that is a habit of mind that had been developed during nearly a decade of ideological struggle against Fascism. The bulk of the British people, one ought to remember, remained anæsthetic to that struggle until late into 1940. Abyssinia, Spain, China, Austria, Czechoslovakia—the long series of crimes and aggressions had simply slid past their consciousness or were dimly noted as quarrels occurring among foreigners and "not our business." One can gauge the general ignorance from the fact that the ordinary Englishman thought of "Fascism" as an exclusively Italian thing and was bewildered when the same word was applied to Germany. And there is nothing in Wodehouse's writings to suggest that he was better informed, or more interested in politics, than the general run of his readers.

The other thing one must remember is that Wodehouse happened to be taken prisoner at just the moment when the war reached its desperate phase. We forget these things now, but until that time feelings about the war had been noticeably tepid. There was hardly any fighting, the Chamberlain Government was unpopular, eminent publicists were hinting that we should make a compromise peace as quickly as possible, trade union and Labour Party branches all over the country were passing anti-war resolutions. Afterwards, of course, things changed. The Army was with difficulty extricated from Dunkirk, France collapsed, Britain was alone, the bombs rained on London, Goebbels announced that Britain was to be "reduced to degradation and poverty." By the middle of 1941 the British people knew what they were up against and feelings against the enemy were far fiercer than before. But Wodehouse had spent the intervening year in internment, and his captors seem to have treated him reasonably well. He had missed the turning-point of the war, and in 1941 he was still reacting in terms of 1939. He was not alone in this. On several occasions about this time the Germans brought captured British soldiers to the microphone, and some of them made remarks at least as tactless as Wodehouse's. They attracted no attention, however. And even an outright Quisling like John Amery was afterwards to arouse much less indignation than Wodehouse had done.

But why? Why should a few rather silly but harmless remarks by an elderly novelist have provoked such an outcry? One has to look for the probable answer amid the dirty requirements of propaganda warfare.

There is one point about the Wodehouse broadcasts that is almost certainly significant—the date. Wodehouse was released two or three days before the invasion of the U.S.S.R., and at a time when the higher ranks of the Nazi party must have known that the invasion was imminent. It was vitally necessary to keep America out of the war as long as possible, and in fact, about this time, the German attitude towards the U.S.A. did become more conciliatory than it had been before. The Germans could hardly hope to defeat Russia, Britain and the U.S.A. in combination, but if they could polish off Russia quickly—and presumably they expected to do so—the Americans might never intervene. The release of Wodehouse was only a minor move, but it was not a bad sop to throw to the American isolationists. He was well known in the United States, and he was—or so the Germans calculated—popular with the Anglophobe public as a caricaturist who made fun of the

silly-ass Englishman with his spats and his monocle. At
the microphone he could be trusted to damage British
prestige in one way or another, while his release would
demonstrate that the Germans were good fellows and knew
how to treat their enemies chivalrously. That presumably
was the calculation, though the fact that Wodehouse was
only broadcasting for about a week suggests that he did
not come up to expectations.

But on the British side similar though opposite calcu-
lations were at work. For the two years following Dunkirk, British morale depended largely upon the feeling
that this was not only a war for democracy but a war
which the common people had to win by their own efforts.
The upper classes were discredited by their appeasement
policy and by the disasters of 1940, and a social levelling
process appeared to be taking place. Patriotism and left-
wing sentiments were associated in the popular mind, and
numerous able journalists were at work to tie the association tighter. Priestley's 1940 broadcasts, and "Cassandra's" articles in the *Daily Mirror*, were good examples of
the demagogic propaganda flourishing at that time. In
this atmosphere, Wodehouse made an ideal whipping-boy.
For it was generally felt that the rich were treacherous,
and Wodehouse—as "Cassandra" vigorously pointed out
in his broadcast—was a rich man. But he was the kind of
rich man who could be attacked with impunity and without risking any damage to the structure of society. To
denounce Wodehouse was not like denouncing, say, Bea-
verbrook. A mere novelist, however large his earnings may
happen to be, is not *of* the possessing class. Even if his

income touches £50,000 a year he has only the outward
semblance of a millionaire. He is a lucky outsider who has
fluked into a fortune—usually a very temporary fortune
—like the winner of the Calcutta Derby Sweep. Consequently, Wodehouse's indiscretion gave a good propaganda opening. It was a chance to "expose" a wealthy
parasite without drawing attention to any of the parasites
who really mattered.

In the desperate circumstances of the time, it was excusable to be angry at what Wodehouse did, but to go on denouncing him three or four years later—and more, to let
an impression remain that he acted with conscious treachery—is not excusable. Few things in this war have been
more morally disgusting than the present hunt after trait-
ors and Quislings. At best it is largely the punishment of
the guilty by the guilty. In France, all kinds of petty rats
—police officials, penny-a-lining journalists, women who
have slept with German soldiers—are hunted down while
almost without exception the big rats escape. In England
the fiercest tirades against Quislings are uttered by Conservatives who were practising appeasement in 1938 and
Communists who were advocating it in 1940. I have striven
to show how the wretched Wodehouse—just because success and expatriation had allowed him to remain mentally
in the Edwardian age—became the *corpus vile* in a propaganda experiment, and I suggest that it is now time to
regard the incident as closed. If Ezra Pound is caught
and shot by the American authorities, it will have the
effect of establishing his reputation as a poet for hundreds
of years; and even in the case of Wodehouse, if we drive

him to retire to the United States and renounce his British citizenship, we shall end by being horribly ashamed of ourselves. Meanwhile, if we really want to punish the people who weakened national morale at critical moments, there are other culprits who are nearer home and better worth chasing.                                    1945.

9 780156 260534